THE BEST OF ASK DANNY 2004

with

THE COLLECTED ESSAYS

THE BEST OF ASK DANNY
2004

with

THE COLLECTED ESSAYS

BY

DANNY CAHILL, CPC
PRESIDENT OF ACCORDINGTODANNY

Foreword by

Danny Sarch, CPC
President, The Pinnacle Society

THE BEST OF ASK DANNY 2004
WITH
COLLECTED ESSAYS

© 2004 by Danny Cahill

AccordingToDanny LLC
781 Highland Avenue
Cheshire, CT 06107
www.accordingtodanny.com

Manufactured in the United States of America
First Edition

TABLE OF CONTENTS

Foreword – Danny Sarch   p. 1

Introduction – Danny Cahill   p. 5

Best of Ask Danny   p. 9

    Candidate Management   p. 11
    Client Issues   p. 27
    Fees   p. 47
    Marketing   p. 59
    Nightmares   p. 75
    Owners and Managers   p. 89
    Recruiting   p.117
    The Recruiting Life   p.133
    Telephone   p.143

Collected Essays   p.163

    Did I Say That Out Loud?   p.167
    You're Just Like Me Only Different   p.177
    Pivotal People   p.181
    Retaining Top Recruiters   p.189
    Gospel of Gossip   p.193
    Brothers Keeper

About the Pinnacle Society   p.197

About Danny Cahill and AccordingToDanny   p.199

FOREWORD

I've known Danny Cahill only since 1999. That's more than a little embarrassing since I'd been working as a headhunter full time since 1984. Embarrassing for me, since for 15 years I did not know that there was this little shadow industry whose sole purpose was to make me better at what I did. Embarrassing for him too - nice marketing effort!

In 1999, *Deconstructing Danny* was shown at a Pinnacle meeting. Other Pinnacle members said glowing things about Mr. Cahill, but, cynic that I was, I started doing my own research. I discovered we had a lot in common. Both of us prefer to be called "Danny" rather than the formal "Daniel." Both of us were English majors in college, had done nothing but headhunting as a career and then bought out our old bosses in our 20's.

I realized very quickly, however; that I was in fact, "Danny Lite." Cahill got a Masters in English Lit; Sarch, a mere Bachelors. Cahill built a big diversified search firm; Sarch, a small highly niched one. Cahill is a nationally renowned, gifted, public speaker; Sarch, a pretty good joke-teller. Cahill has had two wives; Sarch, only one. Cahill is a fitness-obsessed workout fiend; Sarch is in pretty good shape. You get the idea...

I sent Danny an e-mail after that Pinnacle meeting, outlining some of the above, and telling him how I enjoyed his tape. To my surprise, he reached out and called me. And I learned how generous he really is. He also invited me to a gig he was doing in Manhattan. I took my team with me (two other full-time recruiters) and, I got to meet Danny for the first time.

While struggling with a bad leg (which I unabashedly took advantage of the first time we played tennis), Danny gave his typical virtuoso seminar performance. I was struck by how insightful he was, how "real" his stories were, and how

1

funny he was. His gift as a speaker was that he made sure you enjoyed what you were hearing, which inspired remembering what was said, which in terms compels you to implement what he recommends, which in turn **made me more money.**

During the summer of 2000, I paid Danny to formally mentor me. Within the first hours of observing me at work, he had nailed what made me successful in my niche. His insight enables me to this day, to nurture and protect that strength and, in turn, leverage it by teaching it to my people. Again, he **made me more money.**

We've become friends and, I've been in his office many times since, for either a bathroom break on my way to Hartford, or just to get together for lunch. Because of this, I've had the good fortune of watching him in action as a manager of a thriving, vibrant search firm. It's been said that Ted Williams was the "world's best" at three things: fly fishing, flying fighters, and yes, hitting a baseball. If you've only seen Danny give a wonderful seminar or only been mentored by him, you've had two wonderful experiences, but the truth is you have only seen 2/3 of the triangle - it's like you never saw Ted Williams hit a baseball.

Unlike most other trainers, gifted in their own right at speaking and mentoring, Danny still runs a super real-life executive search firm. What he sees every day are actual deals, with all of their ups and downs in a real-life laboratory. One of his gifts is his ability to effectively manage at ground-level while observing all with his wry eye, and retaining it all, from 30,000 feet. Hence the grist for his seminar mills is always fresh, funny, and REAL.

AccordingToDanny gives **every** headhunter the ability to watch our industry's equivalent of seeing Ted Williams hit. You get the chance to have Danny manage you, if only just a little bit. The industry's best mind is available in one place for all of us to pick.

Much of that wit and wisdom is consolidated in this volume. Read it, laugh a little, learn a lot, and best of all, if you take the time to truly implement what he teaches, you will **make more money.**

Danny Sarch
September, 2004

INTRODUCTION

"I'm happy to give you my advice, since I'm not using it at the moment."

Mark Twain

They say you never forget your first. My first "Ask Danny" came over a decade before we ever thought to brand the concept. I was still in the early stages of a speaking career. That is to say, I was doing it for free. It seemed remarkable to me that someone would fly me in and let me talk about my favorite subject...running a recruiting desk, and even more amazing that they would sit and listen. It was clear to me from the feedback I would get at the sessions that we all had similar problems and concerns. Often I would linger in my breakout room hearing about someone's wacky closing scenario which always included some "heartbreaking work of staggering genius," but never became an actual completed deal. Then, the next speaker would clear his throat, tap his watch, and ask me to vacate the premises.

It wasn't long before I would get phone calls, letters, and emails once I got back to my office and began attacking my own desk. They would first praise the seminar, using flattery to build a sense of obligation, and then they would ask me to write a script or suggest an angle with which they could go back in to revive a deal. Since I suffer from a lifelong insatiability for attention and affection, I would call or write back immediately, hoping to come in on my white horse and save the day. When it worked, I felt the endorphin rush of the runner...the speaker's high! As I write, I am looking at the letter I got many years ago from Gail Audibert, a very successful insurance recruiter. She wrote me the first letter and request for help that I can recall. Memory is a kind and docile creature; I'd like to think I helped her, but knowing how little I knew then versus now, let's just say she was taking a risk.

5

When I began years later, to formally mentor some of the world's top producers, Ask Danny was the central way we communicated. Once a week, they would email me their *problem log*, objections that tripped them up, closing problems. I would send back scripts along with the rationale for the script, so that they weren't just parroting my words, but could recreate the script in their own words the next time, much as I manage my own recruiters in my search firm. It became a very effective staple of my mentoring. When we decided to launch AccordingToDanny, and make the mentoring available to the recruiting community at large, we knew Ask Danny would be a focal point.

Some things you should know:

- I answer 80-90% of them. Sometimes it's midnight when I get to the last of them for the day, but I answer them. We have grown so fast that I do delegate some of them to top producers in my office and in the Pinnacle Society that I know have specific expertise. (Some ongoing contributors I'd like to thank include Lisa Iannone, Kendra Cunningham, Amy Williams and Vern Chanski.)

- I don't like getting stumped. So, I will go to great lengths to do research and call my extensive network of staffing experts to get answers. This, to me, is the benefit of membership in AccordingToDanny, and since learning is the key to vitality, I'm happy to do it.

- The Ask Dannys prove a couple of things about our business. 1) It is never boring. 2) People do absurd and insane things. 3) It can be hilarious. 4) It can be enervating and depressing, all on the same day. (Hell, on the same call!!)

- Searching the Ask Danny's via keyword search provides excellent mini training meetings for your people, (as does this book). Reading the new ones that come in weekly will keep you focused and in touch with contemporary issues.

The Ask Dannys tend to fall in one of three overall categories in my mind. Some are "rant" Ask Danny's where you simply want to rail against how unfair life is and how trying running a desk can be. I give you a hard time when you write these, as I would if you worked for me. I think it's a privilege to be in our business, and every day you have an opportunity to do important, noble work that just happens to pay a lot of money. So get over yourself and get back to it. I'm aware that hearing that from me is exactly why some of you write. You have no one to kick your butt. Some Ask Danny's are the opposite. You want to brag. And you have chosen the life of the solo practice, and there is no audience, no slap on the back coming. So you wrap your victory in a question, "I just want your opinion, Danny. Was I right to be so brilliant?" Great recruiters are attention and adrenaline junkies. I am thrilled to be there for you.

And then there are the "rescues." These are the ones I live for. The deal is going south, the patient is in the ambulance, turning blue, and you need a solution RIGHT NOW or last rites are going to be read. Don't get me wrong, I'm not saying I'm some guru that acolytes climb up the mountain to get "The Word" from. It's just a fact that when you are *in* a deal, you can't really *see* the deal. You want or need it too badly. I don't. The nature of Ask Danny is that my clinical, detached view, coupled with some acumen forged in the trenches, and I guess I would have to add immodestly some imagination as far as solutions, allow me to suggest a way out you can't see when it's your money hanging in the balance. Since its inception, we have made hundreds of placements happen for our readers, who by the way have an average fee of $20,000 plus. I'm very proud of our results, and look forward to the next question I see when I go in the office tomorrow.

We also included in this collection the articles that I have written for the Pinnacle Society and other groups. My fondest hope is that you will experience a transfer of passion and enthusiasm from these pages. As I have often noted, there's not much wrong in any of our lives that a placement doesn't fix.

Warm Regards,

Danny Cahill

BEST OF ASK DANNY

CANDIDATE MANAGEMENT

The biggest compliment a recruiter can get is when a candidate, knowing you get paid a fee if he/she takes your offer, still says to you, "What do you think I should do?"

Fear of Change	p. 13
Fear of Change, Part Two	p. 15
Non-competes and the Eulogy Close	p. 18
Relocation Blues	p.20
My Candidate Wants the Other Job I Have	p. 23
Controlling Spouses	p. 25

Fear of Change

Dear Danny:

I have a candidate who has been working at the same company for 25 years; I just got negotiated a 20% raise with a client who wants to hire him.

What ammo can I use to handle the fear of change issue?

AccordingToDanny replies:

My friend, we are swimming upstream on this one. Steel yourself emotionally. I judge your chances of an acceptance, based on what you wrote and our follow up call to you at 80-20 *against!*

Red flags?

1) If he/she were properly pre-closed, you would have a yes or no by now. Today's maybe, is tomorrow's no.
2) Motivation - money is the number one reason people accept counter-offers. 20% to leave, 15-20% to stay?
3) 25 years! Are you kidding me? This is not fear of change. It's paralysis! He/she knows no other home. His/her routines have fossilized; the culture of the current company is indelibly etched into the soul.
4) Divorce. If he/she is going through it or just finished, his/her judgments are not to be trusted. The decision making is faulty and based on fantasy and the lamenting of lost time. They talk about change, but then just before they leap, someone close to them says, *"You've gone through so much, wait until things settle down."*

Sometimes! Sometimes, you get a live one. A relentlessly optimistic person who doesn't feel his/her life is over, and is convinced that patterns can be overcome, and goddamn it, they need a new job and some new friends and change!

You have to make this close emotional. Call him before he turns it down and tell him time kills deals, and you know from experience how hard this is. You want change on a logical, rational level, but the heart whispers, *"What if I'm not any good? What if I get exposed?"* Most people 25 years in one company should stay there, because they can't overcome their fears. But you know what? They get old before their time.

Challenge him. Ask him, **"What would you do if you weren't afraid? If you were unemployed and you interviewed at both my job and the one you've had for 25 years, which one would you want?"** *(If he says yours, you point out that only fear is standing in the way.)*

Ask him if he wants your opinion, knowing that you have a vested interest? Ask him if he trusts you enough to tell him the truth? If he says yes, you say, 'I know how you feel, and it is scary, but others have felt that way, and they found if they make the change it does incredible, life changing things for their spirit, and if they lose nerve and don't make a change, their spirit starts to wither... .I don't want to see that happen... ' "

You can't fight this based on money. You will lose. You can't fight it based on benefits or old technology. He will rationalize a way out. You have to rip open his guts. You have to make him face his own mortality. His personal legacy is at stake. Help him see it.

14

Fear of Change, Part Two

Dear Danny:

This is a follow up to a question regarding getting someone to resign after 28 years at the same company.

Well you were right. The candidate accepted said he was starting and never showed up for his first day.

This has never happened to me before and I'm trying to save face with the client. (The candidate gave a 4 week notice and I warned them about this.) I believe they blame me for this disaster after a long and difficult retained search.

Is there anything I can do to remedy this situation?

I've already sent 3 candidates to interview. (This no-show happened 2 days ago.) The client isn't responding; should I just move on? I'm taking this personally even though I think we did our job and I shouldn't feel this way.

AccordingToDanny replies:

I can't beat you up about this, even though the signs were there, for two reasons.

1) It's happened to me and my recruiters more times than I care to think about.

2) Good recruiters beat themselves up so much it's just no fun.

From the client side, they're reeling. Give them a little time, and they'll come around. If you have three potential replacements, and they're quality replacements, not knee jerks by you, you gently remind them you are being

15

proactive and the sooner they get back on the horse the better.

But, if they're not responding because you felt desperate and wanted to appear like a Canadian Mountie approaching archetypal Nell on the tracks, and sent three decidedly weak resumes, you need to find someone really good. Once you do, and they meet him/her, a lot of the bad feelings will go away. People can fall in love on the rebound, but hell, even a rebound relationship has to be "carom worthy."

So here's a shortcut...go to your shady old veteran of 28 years, the one who broke your heart and didn't show, and put on the guilt trip. Lay it on thick. Make it clear:

1) Your decision has enraged the client.

2) They're taking it out on me.

3) You used me and I hope you get hit by a semi and taste your own blood...

Okay, skip number three...I get a little carried away. But you *can* call him and say his decision has put you in a bind, and now you need his help and he owes you. You want someone as good or better and you want them fast. Don't worry about whether they are looking. You'll determine that. Tell him delicately that you need someone not as far along the Career Arc who still has things to prove and ambition to fulfill, and if he chooses to give you someone in his own company who is angling for his job, well you promise to remove that threat for him and you'll keep it confidential when you make the recruiting call.

If this doesn't work, then go back to targeted recruiting calls. But talk to the client first and make sure they haven't already gone in another direction. If they have you're wasting your time.

And if they have, let it go. Sometimes our product breaks
our heart. But it can also say thank you. Keep that in mind.

Non-competes and the Eulogy Close

Dear Danny:

Aargh!! I just had a candidate turn down an offer because he got nervous about his non-compete. My client's legal counsel has reviewed the agreement (it's a good one) and they have decided that they are willing to take the risk, but they want him to understand that there is inherent risk on his part in violating the agreement. He has a new baby and his wife has decided not to return to work so he's the sole support of the family and nervous about jeopardizing his livelihood. I asked him this question, *"If the non-compete wasn't an issue, and you were interviewing for two jobs, the one with my client and his current position, which would you take?"* He affirmed that if it weren't for the non-compete, he'd accept my client's offer in a heartbeat. Any thoughts or do I just suck it up and move on?

AccordingToDanny replies:

This calls for a **eulogy close**. In the eulogy close, we get away from the specific and go universal, and then we backtrack. Here is what I'd say:

"I appreciate your concern about the non-compete, and we should talk about that risk, because it exists, though not in the worst case scenario your mind is wandering to, but first...

"Can we already write your eulogy? (Wait for answer.) Will you be there your entire life? Will we be able to say 40 years from now he signed a non-compete in 1999 and worked there for the next 34 years, because he didn't want to threaten his family's livelihood? (He'll say no, I promise.)

"So we've established you're leaving. The question is when.

"So now let's talk about threatening your livelihood. The first time I got divorced I nearly didn't do it because of the difficulties in dividing up our stuff. I was 26. We had a stereo and an apartment. She got the stereo, I got the speakers. It's absurd now, but I couldn't see the reality for me then. This is the reality for you now:

"Every year you wait, your young kids will have bigger issues that make it harder for you to risk changing jobs until those issues are resolved. So you wait. And you get resentful. And eventually, you give up, which is sad, or you're so old you're no longer wanted by my clients, which is pathetic. But it happens.

"Here is the real risk of non-competes in dollars and cents. You will potentially get sued. Our client says they will defend. Let's say they renege. (They won't but we're trying to ease your worst case fears.) *The average non-compete adjudicated in the US will cost 10-25K to defend, and because America has increasingly become a 'right to work' nation that frowns on non-competes – they are illegal in California and other states, there is NO risk that you will be kept from working. Even if you lose, you will be forced to not call on certain clients, or not work for 60 days, or not discuss trade secrets for a couple of years. You will not risk unemployment.*

"So if our client is the future, and you see more than 10-25K in personal benefit to you if you went with them, don't blame the noncompete if it's truly lingering fear of change.

At the end of the day, it will be your eulogy. Remember that courage is not the absence of fear. It is the mastery of fear."

That's what I'd try. Meanwhile, I'd be recruiting...

Relocation Blues

Dear Danny:

I have been running into this problem - I have a lot of good jobs that involve relocation. I qualify and re-qualify the candidates on their willingness to relocate. I ask the questions about how the spouse or significant others feel about a move. (By the way, I like the new spouse questions in your recent Ask Danny about Controlling Spouses.) I ask the questions in the Counteroffer Questionnaire.

I do this in the initial candidate interview, before referring a candidate to my client, when I set up an interview, and before setting up any follow up. I try to make the questions sharper as we get closer to the specifics. I don't set up face-to-face meetings for candidates, in my world almost always only after an initial phone interview and after through client and candidate debriefs, who are enthusiastic about the opportunity and who have told me they will relocate to the area in question. Now, this is the problem. In the last month I have had four candidates contact me at the last minute to wave off the face-to-face interviews, one even after the airplane tickets have been purchased. I have egg on my face. My bosses are not happy. They want me to stop working with candidates where a relo is required. Two questions. What is normal in our business for a last minute, *"I talked to "X" and I want to take a pass on this interview?" And what else could I be doing that I'm not doing?*

AccordingToDanny replies:

Your question forces me to make an assumption, but it's a big one. *I'm assuming they are backing out because of the relocation, and not for another reason.* Relocation is often the excuse and not the reason, and you may have a bigger qualifying issue of not drilling down on the seriousness of the candidate to make *any* move. Ask yourself if you really understand their pain, and is that pain urgent enough to make a physical move, which even at its best, if its an area you want to live in, is one big hassle.

But you sound pretty competent to me and comprehensive in your assessments, so let's go with how to better qualify whether someone will move.

Here's the rule: Don't ask them if they're willing to move. Everyone says yes. (Especially the way that most recruiters ask the question, *"For the right opportunity, if the salary was much higher than what you're making, and you had a chance to be the VP in 2 years, would you be ambitious enough to move to eastern Michigan?"*)

You might as well ask them if they love their mothers in front of their mothers. The only answer is yes, unless you want to admit you're a slothful slug who wants to die in your current job.

I don't ask if they will relocate. I ask an open-ended question, *"Tell me about the relocations you've made in your career?"* The best way to predict a person's future behavior is by finding out what their past behavior has been. Did they sell a house? Did they have trouble regrounding the kids in a new school system? Did they live in temp housing for a while? What was that like? Are you willing and ready to go through it again? Some are convincing when they say they know the drill. Some, it's clear, dread it.

Many have to answer the question by saying they've never done it. (But they'll live anywhere, have friends in eastern Michigan, drove through there once in college and had a blast.) Fuhgeddabouditt!! These folks are in for a world of shock and pain, and once they put pencil to paper and realize how much it will cost to sell a house or buy a house, moving Grandma's precious heirlooms, and never again have coffee cake on Sat mornings with their soul mate neighbors, they panic and back out. Then they call you.

21

So explain this to them. The" Post Relocation Conversation Paralysis" that you as a recruiter have to warn them about. Ask them why you should believe they'd be any different. Why would they move?

Happily, there are often reasons. Family in the area. Returning to a change of seasons. Getting the hell out of cold weather. I placed someone who loved the West Coast but wanted his daughters to have the Currier and Ives New England upbringing of his youth, so I targeted New England and found him a job in New Hampshire.

But you have to probe first, measure the concern, and be prepared, more often than not, to not present them and ask for referrals.

My Candidate Wants the Other Job I Have

Dear Danny:

I have a fantastic problem. I was retained to identify and place a sales manager for a brand owned by a larger company. They have a number of similar brands under an umbrella. My client is seen as the No. 1 brand in its field. Recently the parent group bought out another brand which has not performed as well but is still seen as attractive even though they have declined over the past 4 years. I found 2 people and they want to take both on, 1 with my client and the other with their new acquisition. Sounds great but the 2nd chap is not too keen, as he really wants the first role. However, he is willing to meet the new Managing Director for the 2nd firm. I have spoken about plans, challenges, etc. Is there anything else I can do?

AccordingToDanny replies:

That *is* a nice problem to have!!

But it is a problem, because there is emotion here, and emotion is dangerous. He/she feels like the runner up to the real prize, the first job. You've done the hard work, you've gotten him/her to agree to go in and meet the Managing Director with an open mind. Now he/she needs an open heart.

Prep your client that it's only human to feel let down and unloved. It's up to them to reverse these feelings with some TLC (tender, loving, care). Your client must do this, coming from you, they're fairly empty words. Your client must be able to clearly enumerate why the second job is every bit as important.

This is a classic case for a classic close. (And take a look at my Webex on www.accordingtodanny.com called

Objections Overruled.) **Use the objection as the reason for buying!!**

In other words, you close this by saying the reason to take this job is because you weren't right for the other job. The other job is easier to do, that brand is doing well, and it's a maintenance job, requiring less skill and imagination. The second one is harder, riskier and, therefore, **has more recognition and rewards built in if you succeed. No one is impressed with the swimming coach of Michael Phelps. But turn around a loser, the way Bill Parcells did last year, and everyone wants to know how you did it, and will pay you to do it again.**

The other candidate didn't beat you out. They weren't qualified for the tougher job...

Double team this with your client and this close and you should have two placements!! Who is better than you?!

Controlling Spouses

Dear Danny:

My co-workers and I have had a rash of overbearing, over-controlling spouses. From the first call when we run an ad to negotiating salary, these spouses have literally "taken over" the interview process. Despite our efforts to stop them, they make themselves the gatekeepers so we have to involve them in process because we seemingly have no choice!

Please help us!

AccordingToDanny replies:

I have had a rash of an overbearing spouse myself lately, in fact I get a rash just thinking of some of the stuff she's pulled...but I digress.

Look, spouses are always central to candidate's making decisions. It's just that some are more forthcoming about it than others, while others use the spouse as an excuse because it seems unimpeachable - *"I have to do what's right for my family."* I still remember Michael Jordon quitting basketball at age 30. Despite the rumors of gambling abuse, he said he wanted to spend more time with his wife, and then spent the next 5 months playing minor league baseball...

You will never usurp the spouse's power. Why? *Because they can withhold sex!* So it's better to join them.

Make it a part of your standard interview to ask:

"How does your spouse feel about this move?"

"Will your spouse be inconvenienced in any way?" Examples include day care, commute, and the spouse's own job.

"Do they have any misgivings about you moving the process along, or are they asking you to hurry up and get it done?"

Once I measure whether the spouse is friend or foe, I go for the jugular. I say this,

"To work effectively together, it must be collaboration. Part of that collaborative effort includes your spouse. Until I talk to him/her, I'm just the element in your life creating disruption and change. We do a 15 minute call with spouses before we begin contacting our clients on your behalf to introduce ourselves, bring an element of comfort, and often get input from them as to how best to work with you. After all, nobody knows you better. When can I have that conversation with your spouse?"

My experience has been that good candidates see this as a value added service, and bad candidates, the control problems, are scared to death of it. Why? They haven't told their spouse they're looking, that's why.

Do this prep not for all your candidates, but for the ones you send out because you know they're quality fits and will probably get an offer.

CLIENT ISSUES

It's all attitude. A client is nothing more than a candidate with a job.

Fired by My Client   p. 29
Trouble with HR   p. 31
Don't Solicit Our Employees!   p. 33
Large Companies and "You Have to Go to HR"   p. 35
Three Placements and ... Worried about
  Payment   p. 38
My Client Let Confidentiality Slide   p. 40
We Found Him in Our Database   p. 42
What Are We Owed?   p. 45

27

Fired by My Client

Dear Danny:

This past week my firm had a client tell us that they were no longer going to work with us because they had heard from one of our competitors, as well as from a candidate, that their Account Executive (my recruiter) was speaking poorly about the company. My AE swears that she has not said anything negative about the client and I believe her. Your thoughts? I am planning on calling the client to hear it for myself, but I was wondering if you have ever experienced this?

AccordingToDanny replies:

The truth is somewhere in the middle...

That's my credo, my "go to" response for most things in life. So if we apply that dictum here, somewhere between your candidate and client being involved in a conspiracy to smear your recruiter's integrity, which means your recruiter is totally innocent, and the opposite extreme of your recruiter talking out of school and getting busted...is the truth.

I long ago gave up the "CSI" approach of trying to find out who said what and what their various motivations are. They have all had time to create plausible defenses, and this way lies madness.

Assuming you care about this client, you must take action:

1) Call the client. Let them know that you've heard it, don't like it, and will investigate. Assure them you will take appropriate action if it is true, including potentially firing your recruiter. This shows gravitas. Let them freak a little and tell you it's not THAT big a deal.

2) Call the candidate and do the same.

3) Have your recruiter send an email apologizing for the misunderstanding, but don't let her go into some diatribe. Just have her write "My boss is looking into this and very upset. I just wanted you to know it was not my intention and I believe I was misunderstood."

4) Report back to your client. This should be a phone call. Now you clear things up. Now you tell your side. Now you try to persuade based on your findings. If you believe your recruiter was at least partially at fault, offer to remove them as their account executive. But the bottom line is I make it clear I have taken this seriously because I value the client. I have made my recruiter's life a nightmare. It won't happen again. Of course, my recruiter understands this "hyperbolic" strategy going in and is on board with it to save the client as well.

The point is to be empathetic and responsive, not just blindly loyal to your recruiter and deny, deny, deny. I still have, after many years, several clients with whom I have employed this strategy.

You may find that your recruiter has truly been treated poorly and is completely innocent. This is rare (see above credo.)

If that's the case, recruit every last person they have...and feel good doing it...

Trouble with HR

Dear Danny:

We have a client that, up until now has been FANTASTIC.
We have had a GREAT relationship with them. We are the
1st call that HR makes every time and we seem to fill
everything that they need. It is a large insurance company
with 3 locations in our region alone. Everyone wants to work
there for direct hire and everyone wants to work there for
temporary placement. They treat our temps and candidates
with great respect. So...they changed accounting systems
and neglected to tell us that they wanted invoices sent out
differently until they were sitting at 60 days overdue. HR
apologized up and down weekly. We went to A/P and, as it
turned out, I was speaking with the CEO of corporate
accounting. It got back to HR, of course, and she feels that I
went over her head...didn't intend to, but I wanted to try
and help to move the situation move along as we are
talking about $64K or more and much of it now over 90
days. HR told me today that she was going to get a check to
me TODAY and would be ending everyone's temporary
assignments. It is apparent that she will no longer be
working with us. They are approximately 35% of our
business and this would be a terrible loss to us. Any thoughts
on how to remedy this and whether or not you think that it
is even worth a remedy? And if you think that I should
move on, what do I tell my temporary employees that I will
have to let go of today? Should I tell them the truth?

AccordingToDanny replies:

Mark Twain, who we must remember, never had to meet a
temp payroll, said, "Principles are things for the well fed."

Bottom line, much as I hate to say it, if it's 35% of your biz,
you need to placate and placate fast.

People make new decisions based on new information. You need to go back with a purpose. Call whoever has the juice, and ask for a teleconference with HR and Accounting out of respect for the work you've done together because you have a solution. If you get VM, tell them you don't need a check TODAY, you need a call back.

Offer to adjust your payment terms. If the changing of the accounting systems has made your cash management expectations problematic, you will eat some extra time. You value their business, know how to sell their culture, and that is worth the expected value of the monies. Let's let cooler heads prevail and not end temp assignments for people who are doing a good job but are getting caught up in a minor, number crunching snafu. It's not about the quality of your work, or their integrity in paying. It's an accounting/calendar issue.

If you could get them to meet with you and do this live, all the better!!

Now, that is what you do to save this account. Once you do, you take action. You continue to service them, but you get busy replacing this account which now requires you to eat crow and kiss butt even though $64K, 90 days out is outrageous. You have to replace them by making biz dev calls and finding three other players of one third of their size. Why? Because you NEVER want to have one client responsible for 35% of your business. They have you and they exploit you and that's what's happening. Find three other companies that represent 10% of your business each and you'll sleep much better at night.

Do that and one day you can call this client back and say you've thought about it, and you're pulling your temps unless they pay quicker. But you can't afford that now. Remember, the best revenge....is living well.

32

Don't Solicit Our Employees!

Dear Danny:

When a company's HR generalist calls you to tell you not to solicit their employees, what should we say to that generalist and what rights does each party have? When the company calls us, are we required by law not to call in to that firm?

AccordingToDanny replies:

Damn, I wish I could return this call for you. I LOVE these calls.

When an HR person tells me to stop soliciting their folk, I tell them simply:

"I run an ethical practice, and never recruit from my clients. You, having never paid a fee, are not one of them. If there is a current search assignment where we can change that dynamic, let's roll....otherwise, so sorry."

OR (from the great Richie Harris)

"I work with every company. I simply allow you some input as to direction. I would prefer to put people in. But if we can't work together, I take them out."

OR (very recently)

"Rather than waste your time telling me not to recruit from you when you've given me no business reason not to, you should be spending your time keeping your people happy. HR pros in great companies never have to make a request like this. They know their people want to stay put. You've just incented me to recruit from you more often."

A couple of years ago, in Oregon, a company tried to sue a search firm for soliciting. They were unsuccessful, and no state in the union has any law that prohibits it. This is America, people are free to discuss their lives and make choices. That doesn't mean some companies can't make it a fireable offense to take personal calls or be on an Internet site that posts jobs. But you've done nothing wrong that is actionable by making recruiting calls.

Sounds like you hit someone at their core and made them nervous....nice work.

Large Companies and "You Have to Go to HR"

Dear Danny:

I am finding that more and more of my large clients are giving total control to their HR Departments to manage the hiring process. The hiring managers seem to be in the background and HR has power over the process like I have never seen in the past. When I hear of a position or see a posting, I can't get to the hiring authority.

How are your recruiters securing the name of the hiring managers and getting the ear of that person?

Then, how are they not getting referred to HR who then refuses to work with outside search firms?

More and more of my larger clients are hiring recruiters who have failed in the outside world, but can fill the positions if they have an unlimited supply of job orders provided. It takes them forever and I can get the job done much quicker.

I need your advice. Thanks!

AccordingToDanny replies:

You know my motto about giving any control to HR, **Just Say No!** When you can identify and work with the Hiring Authority effectively, there is no need to involve HR. But when you work with *larger* clients, that's more easily said than done.

The larger the company, the more HR departments create internal pressure to keep their operating costs low. They put into effect policies directing that **all** search agency contact and **all** search responsibility **must** go to HR. And there goes your control... The old "Go directly to HR, do not pass Go, do not collect your $30K fee" objection comes at you like a punch in the gut. It isn't something said by a hiring authority to get you off the phone. They think it is the word of God – their CEO – and they live in fear of violating it.

So, you're forced to go to HR. And then the people in HR, as you note, all too often former recruiters who resent your success as someone still in a business where they failed, simply shut you down. With these people, you can use the best sales strategies, positioning and scripting in the world and still get nowhere. So, to solve your problem and keep your sanity, you have two choices:

1. Work with the small to midsize companies within your niche where HR is not the end-all in the screening and hiring process. You get to work directly with the hiring authority, who appreciates your consultative approach to solving his hiring needs and who, over time, will come to think of you as his 'go to guy' when it comes to staffing.

2. And, yes, work with HR. I know it's almost blasphemous coming from me, but we have several recruiters in my firm who have developed excellent relationships with HR within some Fortune 500 Companies. Their secret is to develop relationships at _higher_ levels within HR. VP's in HR certainly don't want to pay a fee for every hire, but they do realize that *sometimes* it's extremely cost effect to pay a fee for a strategically important hire. (And most of them have done it.) A Senior Partner in my firm has an excellent relationship with the Senior VP of HR at a F500 manufacturer. This SVP has an in-house Recruiting Director with 2 in-house recruiters and support staff. The SVP has learned to call our recruiter, and overrule his Recruiting Director, when he knows the search will be very difficult or 'mission critical' to the company.

When his CEO asked him to justify the four fees paid to our agency last year, the SVP was able to compare the tangible factors involved in all the hires by the company last year, primarily based on what each person brought to the company in terms of money made or money saved. Our four placements contributed more to the bottom line than the 23 other salaried hires made by the internal recruiting team! He shared with us his view of successful recruiting. He uses three metrics to measure that success:

1. **Impact and quality of the hire**. Was this person a home run hire? Did he/she immediately affect the department in a positive way?

2. **Speed**. How fast was the person brought on board? There is always a lost opportunity cost when there is no one solving a technical or operational problem or increasing sales.

3. **Cost**. When compared with 1 & 2 above, was it worth it? In his words, *"In the long run, no one remembers the cost of the hire. They remember how good the person was and how quickly they started making contributions."*

If you can develop that kind of relationship with HR, they will lead you to the hiring authorities to fill their staffing needs and you will become a strategic partner with the company rather than one of many vendors.

Three Placements and... Worried About Payment

Dear Danny:

I have a client I have just done 100K with in the last 45 days. It's a software startup (about 8 months old) with no outside funding and VERY little in revenues thus far.

The owner/CEO has another consulting firm he's been running for the past 10 years that is profitable, and so far he's been using cash from his other business to fund the software startup.

All of a sudden, I am terrified as I realize that my placements not only add to fees he owes me, but to large salaries which will now add to his monthly burn rate. I have no idea if/how he can afford both once these senior folks start. He has just recently started looking for Angel funding, but is financing the whole thing himself as of now. We have received no checks from them yet, and my first person hasn't been there 30 days yet. I'm just trying to be proactive. Any thoughts on how to improve my chances of payment?

AccordingToDanny replies:

Congrats! 100K of billings in 45 days is very cool.

I'll answer the question at-hand first, which is how to get proactive about collections ... .BUT... "man up"....I doubt that you're "all of a sudden terrified" about where this new start-up client with very little funding is going to find the cash to pay you. We'll come back to this later.

You said that you have received no checks yet, but the first person hasn't been there 30 days. I'm assuming then, that you gave 30 day payment terms. If this is the case, I would make a call to the CEO reminding him of the due date of the first invoice and measure his response. Now he may say,

"Thanks for the reminder, I'm aware of that", and then you'll just need to hang tight and see if the check arrives on time.

If he cops to a cash flow issue, I would first call him on the carpet for not bringing this up sooner. You've got to make him feel some guilt for negotiating after the fact. (I'm again making an assumption that you had a fee and terms agreement in place.) Also, remind him that his cash flow problem now becomes yours. After a sufficient amount of firm but professional tongue lashing, I would set up a schedule for payment of all the invoices and have him sign the agreement. You'll have the document to fall back on if you need to send this account to collections or take legal action.

Now, back to my initial reaction to your question. I'm sure, at the very least, it crossed your mind when you were taking the searches or at some point during the recruiting process that you may have a collection issue. So, the appropriate time to "get proactive" was before you started the search work.

One way to hedge your bets would be to get high-risk start-up clients on retainer. What we've done in my office is get the client to pay a full fee up front to engage us if there are multiple searches. Once we close a deal, we can then make a judgment on whether or not to continue search work based on our experience to date.

If you can't close on retainer, you need to have a very honest business discussion with the Owner/CEO about how and when you are going to get paid. This is a valid business concern and he or she should respect you as a professional for doing this up front. Again, get an agreement in writing and then recruit with confidence knowing that you'll get paid for your work.

My Client Let Confidentiality Slide

Dear Danny:

I have been in this business a few years. I recruit on a national basis in the legal industry. I just learned that a firm I've been working with for over a year, and have made placements with, let confidentiality slide. I submitted a candidate to this firm and she has just told me that her present employer found out from an attorney who works for my client. I am very angry for this candidate--who is now in trouble at her firm--as well as for myself, because the candidate is understandably furious with me. Any advice?

AccordingToDanny replies:

You absolutely have some exposure here. It sounds like you've made some deals with this client, which I'm sure makes you nervous about rocking the boat, but allow me to scare you a bit so you get your bearings.

She gets fired. She sues her boss for wrongful termination. She sues your client and you. She not only sues for the loss of wages, but a good lawyer would see this as ripe for emotional duress, and would ask for punitive damages. They would ask for millions, and since 99% of firms in our industry carry no more than a million dollars in errors and omissions insurance, (PLEASE tell me you have E&O — Errors and Omissions insurance; if not, get some), you could potentially lose your entire firm. At the very least, you would spend in the high five figures defending yourself.

Obviously this is the very sobering worst case scenario, but I want you thinking with clarity.

Here is what I would do:

1) Offer to help your candidate by talking to her boss, and saying you directly recruited him/her. He/She was not looking and it's your job to push candidates to shop. He/she might not want this help, but you want to be on record trying to fix this.
2) Insist on a meeting with your client to discuss this. Scare them as I just scared you. Get on record. Send an Email exposing the loose cannon who sold your candidate out. Show great umbrage! You want to be able to prove in court through your documentation, and hopefully their admission, that they caused it, not you.
3) At the meeting, I would push real, real hard for them to understand that if she gets fired due to their screw up, they had better hire her pronto; I don't care whether there is an opening or not. Save yourself tons of money in court and hire her!

And don't forget to charge a full fee. You did nothing wrong.

We Found Him in Our Database

Dear Danny:

I have a client who has been a steady amount of business, is viewed as a strong company to work for locally, and typically presents interesting opportunities for new employees, etc. Over the years I have lost a few deals to them because they store every candidate they've ever received from newspaper ads, Website postings, agencies, etc. in an internal database.

Well, I want to address this "system" up front this time around. I was entrusted with a job opportunity yesterday and already have spoken to a few potential candidates for this new opportunity who have not been contacted or talked to this client ever, who but submitted their resumes there over 2 years ago.

How do you recommend we proceed? I don't enjoy being their red flag for candidates whose skills have advanced, who are currently looking, etc.

AccordingToDanny replies:

Addressing this system up front needs to begin before you pick up the phone and make ANY calls on searches. Your recruiting "ROE" (Rules Of Engagement) need to be clear in the call when you take the job order, in other words, you dictate how you work, not the other way around. This is critical in establishing control of the process overall, not just in the question that you are posing here.

Before you make any more calls on this search, stop, pick up the phone, and call your hiring authority. Explain that you are committed to getting the right people in front of them and want to make sure that the two of you are on the same page as far as sourcing/recruiting candidates is concerned.

42

Let me back up a bit. In taking the job order, you must ask them some key questions about their pipeline and the candidates they have in the loop right now. How much work have they completed to date? Who have they talked to already? Frame these in a way that makes it clear to them that you just don't want to get redundant with your results.

Tell them that your job is more than just identifying talent. It's getting candidates interested, vetting their <u>current</u> (*This is important: emphasize that people's skill sets change. Someone who wasn't qualified 2 years ago could be qualified today.*) skill sets, measuring their counteroffer risk. This all takes time. The front-end process that you run candidates through saves your client time because they talk to candidates only after they have been thoroughly qualified. Explain to them that all of this is done before you even mention the name of any search you are working on. The last thing you want is for your client to be inundated with calls from candidates you deemed unqualified, but who think that they are. Remind them that that's why they pay a fee. Explain to them you work under the assumption that they have exhausted their in-house resources and are now at a point where they need your dedicated help. That being said, <u>anyone</u> you source and get interested in this opportunity, you will get paid for.

You will, by this point, have already had them say to you that a) they need outside help, b) they need you to work on this, and c) they have exhausted their internal resources.

They are coming to you because they need more than just a resume database. You don't have the time to waste getting people updated and interested only to find that four years ago they responded to an ad and won't pay you for the work you have done for them.

What Are We Owed?

Dear Danny:

I submitted a candidate to a client I have made a placement with before.

The client called me with a newly created position to work on.

After a lot of man hours, we submitted a high demand candidate (small supply).

I finally got a response from HR saying they had already set up an interview after realizing they had her resume (which they may have had since they had her contact info).

It seems to me, given the timeline, they contacted her after we submitted her resume.

The candidate didn't know about the position until we told her about it.

If they hire her, do I have any entitlement to the fee?

We have a signed fee agreement.

My gut is telling me they went around us.

What do you think?

AccordingToDanny to replies:

Were this to go to court, you would not have a legal leg to stand on. The "procuring cause" law that is the precedent the system keeps returning to expressly requires you to have arranged an interview. Submittals alone are not enough.

But that is the letter of the law. The *spirit* of the law is intended to protect the agent that created the referral, which in this case you have logical reason to believe is you. Keep quiet about how shaky your legal case is and call the company, review the timeline of events, and tell them that your candidate was unaware of the opening until you called, qualified and created interest, then and ask your company this:

"You're a client and I want to have an ongoing relationship, I don't want a legal battle, and yet I don't feel comfortable letting this go. I will be paranoid about every submittal. If you were me, can you see how it appears I have done a lot of work that I will not get paid for? When I submit a resume a certain amount of trust is involved. It's a fragile system. I don't want to have to block out contact info and refuse to give you names.

Without me this interview would not be happening. Are you really comfortable with me earning nothing in this situation should you hire the candidate?"

And then wait. Shut the hell up!

In the real world you will no doubt have to settle. Anything near half the fee is worthwhile. (You'll lose the case if it goes to court and you'll pay $5K to a lawyer for the privilege.)

Next time, don't get off the phone without setting up the interview. Push!!

(If it's any solace, I had this scenario yesterday and settled for $10K on a fee that would normally be $ 16.5K, and my case was as weak as yours.)

Thank God my mother taught me how to transfer guilt!!

FEE$

"You don't earn your fee for the candidate you send, you earn it for all the candidates you chose not to send."

Flat Rate for Exclusives?   p. 49
They Agreed to the Fee... now...   p. 51
Getting Stiffed   p.53
Fees a la carte?   p. 55
Volume Discount?   p. 57

Flat Rate for Exclusives?

Dear Danny:

My firm has a fantastic opportunity to be the exclusive recruiters for a new medical/surgicenter opening. We've been asked to recruit for physicians, nursing, radiology techs (all modalities) pharmacists, etc., etc., etc. The center is very progressive - modeling their site after Mayo clinic. They also would like us to be able to work with other MD offices that will occupy space to fill their needs as well. If any other recruiters call, they will be funneled to us.

They have asked me to prepare a proposal. I'm curious how you would recommend setting up the fee arrangement? They would like flat rates, and will pay within 10 days of start.

They have also asked me to consider a space at their site, a satellite office where we can serve the needs of the growing center. I'm considering including the cost of the rent/related expenses of the new office in my proposal. HELP. We are excited, but also want to set this up right. Would you offer a flat rate of XX for MD's and XX for others? Or make it so it is based on the amount of salary, with a discount off of our normal 30%, based on the number of hires per month (or per quarter)? Thanks so much for your help!

AccordingToDanny replies:

First of all, congrats on the opportunity. It sounds AWESOME.

But let's keep our heads. One of our Pinnacle members had one of these relationships and it became a nightmare. It's a hard transition for a previously "hunterish" search firm to suddenly be in captivity. You will lose a sense of control, but

hopefully this will be more than made up for in revenue!!
There are a couple of models that work:

A full "on site" relationship, also known as a managed
agency agreement. One of your employees works at the
client's site to better handle process, sits in on staffing
discussions, and builds job orders from the inside out. The
interviews take place through that individual, and they
guide the process. Have the right person on site, and you
can make a lot of money.

You would charge: salary and expenses of the On Site
employee on an ongoing basis, with a 20-30% mark up.
You would reduce your fees to (your call) 20-25%. They
would agree to send all other recruiters through you. If they
did hire through another source other than their own
internal referrals, you would charge half of one fee. If I were
you, I would send other agencies' people only as a last resort,
depending on the size of this account, since you will have to
split the fee.

The more conventional approach is a "blanket retainer"
relationship. They pay you an amount (again tied to the
amount of business. ($200K in potential fees, I would ask for
$25K upfront.) This commits you to working for them
exclusively and is a one year commitment. In addition, they
get a break on each individual placement, (again your call,
20-25%) The same tenets apply. No other sources, you
handle all inquiries, if violated, they pay you one half of one
fee.

Even if you opt for the blanket approach, show them value
by visiting them often. Ask to sit in long-term strategy
meetings that might affect staffing. Offer to supply business
intelligence from the competitors you will be recruiting from.
Do this and they will renew every year. A few accounts like
this and you will be in Pinnacle in no time.

They Agreed to the Fee... now...

Dear Danny:

Back in May, I had a hiring manager call me. He said that he wanted our help. According to him, his company had a big push to hire people who sell equities to smaller institutions. We did a good job qualifying the search. We asked whether our usual fee structure applied (we have a signed contract) and were assured that it did.

They met my candidate and loved him. The candidate loved them. The interviewing process was prolonged due to hiring freezes, layoffs, etc, but the candidate does start today. Our introduction is unquestioned and our involvement kept the guy alive during a very long "we don't know what the delay is" period.

Of course, sometime about a month after we made the introduction, they said that *their* policy is not to pay on this type of hire, at all. They then said they'd pay a flat rate $10k, then a flat rate $20k. I'm told by the hiring manager that $25k was approved, far better than nothing, but far less than we expected.

We placed 19 people with them last year; I want to press the issue. Any thoughts?

AccordingToDanny replies:

You say a month after your introduction you were told of the new fee policy, and voiced concern. But you let the process go on and lost your big stick of stopping the hire until it was resolved. Once he's on board lots of leverage goes away.

But enough hindsight. What you do now depends on how

much of an actor you can be, and how much you're willing to risk. There is a very low probability that you could lose the account but it's a slight possibility. More likely the worst thing that happens is that after the heat of battle, cooler heads prevail. That said, what I would do is a two call close.

Call One: "The Lose Your Mind" Call. The high road of integrity and principle. You guys are squeezing me after the fact, you're taking advantage of the fact you're a key client, negotiating the price after the deal is done in their world ends up on CNBC and in SEC hearings, etc, etc. ... You owe me the whole fee, end of story. I don't care if we never do biz again. It's all or nothing...get off the phone without being apologetic...

Call Two, a few (painful) hours later. (Often they call back first. If they call back it's to tell you they'll pay your fee but your relationship is over...proceed with the next part.) You call and tell them you're sorry. NOT for WHAT you said, but for HOW you said it. It was emotion, you're a passionate guy; you lose it when you feel you're wronged. It's an issue you need to address someday therapeutically. In the meantime, while you believe everything you said in the last call, you now throw yourself on your sword. You want and think you deserve the full fee, but in the spirit of maintaining a good relationship, you'll accept whatever they feel is right.

In my experience, they come in 50-70% of full fee.....

Getting Stiffed

Dear Danny:

How do I get an ex-candidate (successfully placed 7 years ago), now the CEO of a software firm, who has signed a retained search agreement (with my firm) that spells out 3 retainer payments AND a mutually exclusive relationship, to pay the final 3rd payment after they hired an unsolicited referral, a candidate that we were in contact with, through a contingency firm?

AccordingToDanny replies:

In regards to this specific question, I need to know the whole situation. You mention that you were in contact with the other candidate. Did you originally present him/her? Did you schedule an interview? Did you get them interested in the job or did the other firm? Have you already addressed this with them and if so, what was the feedback? Where is this now? In reality, you will have a very hard time fighting this in court or even with your client because the fact is you are really the one that comes out ahead. You were paid 2/3rd's of a fee for a search you didn't fill. If they are willing to pay a full fee to another firm on top of what they already doled out to you, they are the one out a fair amount of extra money - not you.

Suggest to them that instead of paying the remaining third for that search, they roll it over to another search within the organization. Be sure to emphasize that this is an exclusive relationship and that in the future, they not only should, but must refer to you any other firms that have potential candidates, or potential candidates who come to them regardless of source.

I am fully aware that a contract is a contract. But let's be realistic here. It would cost you more to take any legal action than you would ever recoup and again, in this situation you are already coming out pretty unscathed. If you make a big enough issue out of this with your client, that might be one of the things that they come back to you with and they might try to get a refund.

I would be more concerned about the fact that you knew of this candidate and weren't the procuring cause of getting him involved with your client.

In short, choose your battles. If this is a client that you want to keep a relationship with, be flexible. It will be appreciated and will foster loyalty in future dealings.

Fees – a la Carte?

Dear Danny:

I was recently talking with an Angel Funding/Venture Capital/Incubator company who approached me and they flat-out said that my fees are too expensive for their portfolio companies and that a company with less than a million dollars in capital frankly wouldn't use my services. I understand that objection. It makes sense to me.

Is there any way to make money with companies that really won't pay full fees? If I insist on full fees, I'll get nothing.

The Angel Funding CEO and I had the idea that I could offer a menu of services and have these companies pick the services and their fees based on what services they would like...

For example:

> Find resumes 5%
> Screen candidate 5%
> Test candidate 5%
> Check references 5%
> etc...

Is this menu of services a good/bad idea? Is it worth it?

AccordingToDanny replies:

In 1983, just before his death, I went to a Q&A in NYC given by Cary Grant. When asked about the wisdom he had acquired in 80 years on the planet, he said, "There are some advantages to aging. I just can't think of any."

That said, this "menu idea", often called "unbundling," sometimes called "managed agency agreements," predictably comes up in every bad market for a simple and exquisitely sad reason: we are needy, and they can smell it. So we take a crumb. And give it a name to hide our shame.

You will work just as hard producing your work for 5%, you will never get their business at higher levels when the economy turns, and more importantly, you won't feel good about it.

Volume Discount?

Dear Danny:

I have a client asking for a volume discount, i.e. after his third hire can he get a 5% discount? I do not want to compromise because they have another agency on the same positions, but I also want to secure more than three of the ten openings. Suggestions?

AccordingToDanny replies:

To paraphrase an unfortunate time in former President Clinton's vainglorious past, "it depends on what the meaning of the word 5% is."

If it's what I think it is, you charge 30% for the first two deals and 25% for the third, that's not a good solution. Why?

Because it's not 5%....at, say $75,000, your 30% fee is $22,500. At 25% the fee is $18,750...a difference of $3,750. You want to negotiate a deal where you agree to take 5% "off of the total fee" so that at $22,500, you bill them for $22,500 minus-$1125 = fee of $21,375.

If they agree to that, you can even sweeten the deal and take 5% "off of the total fee" starting at deal #1. Remember, you want to create the illusion that they are in control, and that you are operating under the spirit of compromise.

Another approach (go to the AccordingToDanny Training Library for phraseology under "Fees") that would work here is the "sliding scale approach".

They pay full fee for Deal One (say 30%). They then subtract 1% off of the full fee for every successive deal for a one year period.

In this way they earn their discount based on their growing value as a client. There is nothing wrong in the abstract with pricing considerations for clients, but most recruiters, desperate for deals, treat mere customers as clients, give away the store, and sadly, never deal with them again, or worse, continue to work under recessionary pricing all the way through an "up" market, which we are beginning to experience.

Good luck. And hang tough!

MARKETING

"Marketing is not about brilliant, glib scripts. It's about discipline. A high call level with decent selling skills beats a lazy witty wordsmith all day long."

No "Rusing" – But How Do New People
   Get Names?   p. 61
How Do I Ask for Names?   p. 64
There are Only So Many Places to Call   p. 66
Still Working the Good Ole Boy Network p. 68
National Contracts/Local Firms   p. 70
My Candidate Asked Me to Call   p. 72
Presenting at the Top   p. 74

No "Rusing" — But How Do New People Get Names?

Dear Danny:

You have stated that "rusing" is a no-no. The only non-rusing techniques I have heard of are "be very friendly with the gatekeeper, and dazzle her with double talk before getting the name you want." Or, act like you're a moron and forgot who you were calling. You don't spend much time on "name gathering". I think it's the toughest thing to do for a new person. HELP ME!

AccordingToDanny replies:

Ouch, dude, now I know what John Kerry must have felt like last week when Zell Miller, a Democrat speaking at the Republican National Convention, accused Kerry of flip-flopping. Not only was Miller a little like the pot calling the kettle black, but the next day the media claimed Kerry never said the things Miller quoted.

Dazzling with double talk and acting like a moron are not exactly fair characterizations of our "technique" in getting past the gatekeeper. You're referring to my belief that there are two tones of voice, two attitudes that I have found, (and hear over and over again as I review the calls of successful recruiters) are effective.

1) Treating the gatekeeper humanisticly and with courtesy (a little charm doesn't hurt), and 2) having a slightly harried, busy sense (and enough technospeak to make him/her feel compelled to transfer rather than dally).

Okay, I'll stop being defensive now...in fact you are right that what was once a huge part of our training, how to get past the gatekeeper, has been reduced dramatically. Why?

61

Nearly all of the database tools commonly used by the staffing industry include names, titles, even the URL's of enough people inside nearly every company for you to penetrate without ever having to deal with the main gatekeeper.

Much of your problem goes away if you invest in, (and I have no interest in any of these, I'm merely a customer) Hoover's, Data Source, Corp Tech, Elyion Technologies, Broadlook, and even the traditional Boards like Monster and Careerbuilder...

Remember, the point is to get a name inside a company so that you can get past the main gatekeeper, and then the skill you have to hone is being bounced to the party you want. Learning how, when you get the "wrong" person, to apologize and ask for help, *"Oops, my error, Alan, I was trying to get over to someone in manufacturing engineering, do you know who handles tool design on the progressive side?"*

When you have a name off of a Monster or Careerbuilder resume for someone who would be the "boss" of the person you are looking for, *"Hi, can you switch me to Jerry Caldwell? Oh you know what, it might make more sense if I spoke to one of his second in commands, the ones who do the real work. Do you know who in accounting reports to Jerry?"*

Or go to "Jerry" and make an indirect pitch for a referral. The point is the name off the Internet gets you past the toughest sentry. Once you are inside, people assume you know why you are there. It is not rusing not to disavow that notion.

Remember too, that safe areas, like accounting, help desk, inside sales, purchasing, are all areas where you will not get the third degree from the gatekeeper, and you can often get names for people in other departments by going there.

Rusing is lying. Lying erodes the soul. The top producers I
know don't do it, and sleep better. (Maybe that's because
they can afford those really nice, cozy beds.)

How Do I Ask for Names?

Dear Danny:

In trying to get the names of sales people, I'm being put through to the "Inside sales person" who is a very hard screen to get past. Any thoughts on how to deal with handling that?

AccordingToDanny replies:

Because your question is so specific to sourcing names for inside sales, I did something special for you. I went to The Source. Our version of the Oracle at Delphi, our senior researcher, is Jen, who, after six years of sourcing for sales people, can literally get names out of inanimate objects. Here is what she suggests: no fluff, just the facts....

I avoid inside sales the way our recruiters avoid HR. Inside sales is the *end* of the sourcing call, not the beginning.

Why?

Inside salespeople want to get credit for the lead so they're qualifying like crazy. This leads to either you admitting you're from a search firm or them figuring it out pretty quickly. Bottom line: they won't give up their outside people.

So how do you go about getting names?

Be very specific in asking the receptionist for "outside" or "field sales". For example, if you're calling Massachusetts Corporate and you don't care where in Massachusetts you get someone, then use a specific city name: *"Who's your outside or field rep covering Boston?"*

Or use a specific product: *"Who's your field rep selling the document management software to Boston customers?"*

If you're calling HQs in one state but want to get a hold of a rep in another state, try: *"Do you have a 'remote' location on the West Coast?"*

Get the phone number for the remote office and follow up with: *"Who's the field rep out there?"*

Nine times out of ten the remote location only has one guy and he is in outside sales. The receptionist might not even know it.

In a case where the receptionist does not know who handles outside sales or where any other offices are, ask for a Sales Admin or a Sales Coordinator — they are most helpful! And go through the same questions listed above.

Happy hunting!

There Are Only So Many Places to Call

Dear Danny:

Many of our searches are with skilled nursing homes in very remote locations. We cannot find 100 competitors to call. In some cases going out 40 miles we might find 25 competitors. Nurses don't relocate easily so going out longer distances doesn't make a lot of sense. We have determined once we have contacted those limited number of competitors we move on to other searches.

Please let me know your thoughts:

1) Do you agree with our approach?
2) Are there other ways for us to look at the assignment?
3) If it doesn't meet some of our criteria, do we still spend time on the search or do we just keep marketing?

AccordingToDanny replies:

One of the hardest things we face as recruiters is when to abandon hope. We are optimistic by nature, resilient of character, and we hate giving up on any search.

And...oh yeah, we hate making cold calls to get another search.

So we rationalize, we cut deals within our own minds. We compromise. But the top producers I work with are ruthless when it comes to assessing the facts, and they act accordingly.

The facts as you present them:

1) A small universe from which to operate
2) Remote locations

3) The heightened unwillingness to relocate that nursing is known for.

These are not trivial and will not be solved by some minor increase in compensation or the powerful, engaging personality of some hiring authority. They are market realities. You would be well served to accept them, and move on.

You have to find searches where the probabilities of making a deal are enhanced. A lesser position in a metro area where there is urgency may not give you the "Jason and the Argonauts/Golden Fleece" satisfaction that filling one of these jobs might. But you'll make more money, on a more consistent basis, with less stress.

It's one thing not to pick the low hanging fruit, quite another to pass up fruit and insist on seeing the view at the top of the tree. The purpose is to eat, not climb.

Still Working the Good Ole Boy Network

Dear Danny:

For the last 1.5 years I have been responsible for Business Development. The market in Tucson is 90% Good Ole Boy network. I have spent many days visiting from clients and prospects and bringing them freshly baked cookies. The results have been positive and orders have come our way. Recently we have decided to focus on a more consultative sales approach. This approach is appointment-based. My concern is that I will not get the opportunity to visit with some of th e buying influences that are used to seeing me once or twice a month. My fear is this will result in a loss of business because of the lack of face time. Any suggestions on how to not lose this business? I have seen a slight dip in the last two weeks since I stopped the frequent call approach.

AccordingToDanny replies:

Has it been just your face that has gotten the job orders? And is it seeing your face that gets repeat business? My guess is that no is the answer to both questions.

Our experience has been that the recruiting business is about results. What you've not mentioned in your question is how reactive and productive you've been in working these accounts. You may have used a face-to-face, gift-giving approach to winning new business, but trust me, the continuation of those relationships came from the successful filling of their searches. If your clients are well served with good hires, you won't lose them because of less face time.

And the way you have done business in the past worked because that is what it seemed to take to develop your temp business. As I understand it, you are the on the perm side for your company. Frankly, to differentiate your temp division from your perm division, you **have to** act differently, and in your case more professionally. The consultative approach in general, and the marketing and recruiting methodologies we teach, in particular, will be key to that.

For you, the challenge becomes how to replace the pipeline of new prospects as you learn to create a more consultative approach. Face time and gifts may help you break the door down and get a shot, but so will an approach that drills deeply into a company's business pains, the why's and how's of the needs for human talent. The benefit of a consultative approach is that you will be able to refer to what you've learned and ultimately, you will be perceived as a consultant. You will be aware of upcoming growth patterns and not just instantaneous vacancies. There is added value here, in my opinion, more value than a box of freshly baked cookies. Now, if you need a place to send those cookies– visit our CONTACT US page...

National Contracts/Local Firms

Dear Danny:

My firm is a small permanent search firm, specializing in Administrative Staffing. We do no temporary staffing. We work with many Government Affairs offices and local offices of large corporations who have their corporate offices in other parts of th e country. The headquarters of these companies have national contracts with staffing firms and want the DC locations to use them. My local clients find it very frustrating to use these firms, but have a difficult time getting around them, even though the headquarters have been made aware of the difficulty these national firms have in filling these DC positions. Any suggestions on how to overcome this objection?

AccordingToDanny replies:

There are a few strategies that I would suggest.

In your question, you say that you "work" with Government Affairs and local offices of large corporations. My assumption is that you've done business successfully with these clients in the past and the national contacts have been recently put into place. I would certainly get those hiring managers on your side and suggest a conference call with the "Contract" decision makers. If those managers will be on those calls with you, you'll have a much better chance of winning back business. You could potentially build a case that there are specific qualities and therefore a specific qualification process needed for DC-based candidates due to the volume of Government work, and your firm, because of its location, is uniquely positioned to effectively fill these searches.

Do you know if these contracts are general retainers or carry any exclusivity clauses which would mean double fees paid if one of your clients hired from a firm not under contract? If neither of these conditions exists, this may be your way back in at this point. Another contract point to check into is if there are any time restraints put on those firms to produce viable candidates or a hire on a position within a certain time of being given the search. In other words, they may have only 30 days to produce and then you would have the opportunity to work the search.

Ask the corporate contacts for the chance to compete on the very toughest searches, those that no one else has come close on in order to prove the value that your firm would bring.

As a last resort, you could talk with the firms who have the National Contracts and offer to do split business if it means that much to you to be a part of the search work done for those companies.

Failing all these things, remember the old adage, "There are plenty of fish in the sea." I would go after new clients and use the companies that refused to work with me as source companies for the new clients.

Good Luck!

My Candidate Asked Me To Call

Dear Danny:

A candidate of mine has approached me to ask if we would introduce him to a particular company. The company is not currently a client of ours. He saw a posting and, according to his resume he appears to be qualified. Since I don't know the company, I can't know if the chemistry or fit would be right, but I want to get in the door. What do I do?

AccordingToDanny replies:

When this scenario first happened to me years ago, the approach I fashioned worked so well that it has become one of the signature marketing methods of my search firm, one that we discuss in detail in our video series, Marketing Matters (available at www.accordingtodanny.com/store). Instead of pretending we got the lead on our own, or making a conventional marketing call to the client, we use and showcase the candidate's participation.

As in:

"Mr./Ms. _____, this is Danny Cahill, I'm a headhunter and the managing partner of one of the country's oldest and largest privately held search firms, and I focus exclusively in _____ (their niche). I know you get these calls, but I work very differently than my competition. When I work with a candidate they have to provide with me two things: one, a demonstrated track record that makes them elite compared to others who do what they do, and two, they have to know what they want, and prove it by providing me with names of companies they want to work for, and companies where because of their structure or business model they believe they can make an immediate and significant contribution. I'm working with a candidate who qualifies and had you on *their short list of companies she/he asked me to reach out to."*

Then you shut up. They will ask you why the candidate chose them, and you can then start to sell, or they will simply acknowledge that they understand, and you begin making a short, bullet point presentation of your candidate's track record.

Most of my recruiters use this approach, and it's not just salesmanship. We ask our candidates to think about who they want to work for and where they would fit in, and **why!**

Their answers shape and inform the verbiage in our pitch....it's a simple business....

Presenting at the Top

Dear Danny:

I know that I have to be calling more CEOs, presidents, and CFOs. Would you have any good ideas on how to present a senior level candidate (MPC* material) directly to a CEO or president? It's been difficult trying to get past the gatekeeper and she is an invoice waiting to happen.

AccordingToDanny replies:

Two thoughts:

1) Studies show these Big Shots are in the office early and late (but their admins are not). Take two days a week and start work at 7:30 a.m., call just CEOs and presidents, and by 9:00 a.m. you will have talked to more of them than you would in a week of doing it the other way.

2) Your approach should not be submissive or apologetic. It's not, "Thank you so much for giving me your precious presidential time." It's *"Look, I ONLY make these calls when the track record of my candidate demands it.   Prepare to be impressed..."* (and then deliver the goods!!)

* MPC — Most Placeable Candidate — a candidate who is the best possible representative of who you are and the value you bring to your clients.

NIGHTMARES

"The despair I can take; it's the hope that's killing me."

Won't Pay – Won't Call Back   p. 77
I Think They Hired Around Us   p. 79
More Punishment – More Nonpayment   p. 82
He Wants Out... I am Working on More
    for the Company   p. 85

Won't Pay – Won't Call Back

Dear Danny:

I am having the worst problem with a hospital that I recently placed somebody with. The problem is that not only are they NOT paying me but NOBODY is calling me back. I call accounts payable, the controller, the CFO, the CEO, the COO and nobody is returning my calls. I am VERY close to retaining a lawyer but will only do that as a last resort. I call the hospital every day. Should I send a certified letter? Should I have a lawyer handle it? I am absolutely baffled.

AccordingToDanny replies:

Your instinct not to get a lawyer involved is sound. They will take a third and not move very quickly.

A better alternative is to get aligned with a good collection agency that works on a strictly commission basis. They often will work for 25% of monies recovered, but more importantly, they will be indefatigable pests!! They will call every day, twice a day, and put some real meaning into the aphorism: the squeaky wheel gets the grease.

But don't even do that yet.

1) Call your candidate. Explain that you are just trying to give them a heads up and fair warning. You haven't been paid. That generally means the company is not happy with the candidate, and therefore are not paying because they know they are going to let the candidate go. Advise them to go to their boss and ask flat out if they are in trouble. If they get released, you'll be happy to help, but ethics do not allow you to work with them yet, as they are still there. But when there is an

77

overdue bill and no communication? A bad, bad sign, Mr./Ms. Candidate!

This will get you a call back. They will be irritated that you embarrassed them, and angry that you used such a ploy, forcing them to reassure the candidate when it has nothing to do with them. You stand strong. They left you no choice. They were being unprofessional by not calling back, and it often DOES spell doom for the candidate. To use Glen Close's line from Fatal Attraction, "I will not be ignored."

By the way, they will reassure the candidate by promising to pay. And then they will do it.

I Think They Hired Around Us

Dear Danny:

Last August, an employee of mine received a job order from a hospital in California. He was dealing with a director in the operating room. At first, they were looking for somebody who had received their Masters; however, I had just recruited a great local candidate who was taking Masters' classes so I instructed my recruiter to send the resume. He sent the resume and client passed on this candidate.

I have just learned that the hospital hired this candidate through another source, bypassing us. I don't know if they did it intentionally or not, however, we have the faxed resume and the confirmation it was sent on August, as well a and a signed contract specifically stating that if the hospital hires one of our candidates within a year of us submitting a resume, they owe us a fee. Also, during this time the hiring was transferred from one director to another. We did not resend the resume to the new hiring authority because they already told us they were going to pass on our candidate. And obviously, as recruiters, our clients would not like it if we kept resending resumes of candidates they pass on. They made it quite clear that they did not want to talk to our person. We are in the process of calling them now (we have left 2 messages for the hiring authority), but I would like your opinion as to how to handle this.

AccordingToDanny replies:

I was about to send you a sad "Dear John" letter, where I have to tell you that the law is not on your side.

The "procuring cause" rule that governs these events always comes down on 1) the side of the agency that created the action that led to the hire, in your case, the other firm, and

79

2) it recognizes only "interviews" not resumes being sent. In most cases, you would be completely out of luck.

But...lookie here!! You have a contract that states that if the hospital hires someone that you can prove you sent a resume on first you get a fee? Good for you. (Shame on them, I would never have signed that document in a world of Internet resumes that can be downloaded for free.)

So since the spirit of the agreement is to reward the person who first referred the candidate, you need to forget about procuring cause and talk contract.

Here is how you handle this call. You calm down, do some Pilates or something, you do not scream or yell or erupt in a burst of integrity. That comes later and only if you need it. You:

1) Call, and if you get a voice mail, make it clear you have uncovered a serious mistake and one that could have legal ramifications, although you're sure it's a misunderstanding that can be put to bed. This will get a call back. If it doesn't, go over their heads.

2) When you get them, you again assure them you are not impugning anyone's integrity, resumes get lost, people make mistakes, but we have a contract. Here is what it states, and you have hired our guy. (MAKE NO MENTION OF THE OTHER FIRM, NOT YOUR PROBLEM.)

3) Be assumptive. You didn't want to just send a bill without talking to them, but you assume you can now send it along. What is the salary they agreed on, when did he/she start, so we can begin calculating our guarantee period?

Now if this works, great. But it probably won't. It's an opening salvo. They'll talk about how the job changed, the administrator was a different individual, and they went through another agency. Hear them out, tell them you can appreciate it all, but that is why you have a contract. You did your job, saw the match, engaged the candidate's interest, and now expect to get paid. Stay steadfast, and get off the phone if they get hot. If they say they won't work with you again, calmly tell them they're not working with you now if they are going to take your people without paying for them, and you can't believe they feel good about this. Then send the bill. Full Fee. Due ASAP.

In reality, this is a bluff. I don't care what contract you have. No judge is going to find the other agency doesn't deserve this fee. I would wait 3 days and then go back with a settlement offer to preserve the relationship. I would offer to take half the fee in return for an exclusive on another search. When they factor in legal fees, this is a good deal. For you it's an excellent deal because taking this to court (which I deem it too weak to do) would take three years.

How well do you do at the casinos? Your skill is about to be tested...good luck.

More Punishment — More Nonpayment

Dear Danny:

We placed 3 specific individuals with an electronics firm that was quite particular as to what candidates they wanted (and naturally, they wanted people ASAP). Of the 3 hires, the last 2 candidates have already left. One lasted 3 weeks, and said all of a sudden that they were going to start up a restaurant with their fiancée. On this one, the client called BEFORE we received the cheque and said essentially they were going to hold off paying it until a replacement was found. Then, THEY decided to compete with us - and they "found" someone themselves. (No $ for us.)

The second candidate leaving stayed for 4 months (we DID get paid on this one) and she received an offer for $ 20K MORE money and a management role. She told our client in the exit interview that she had been looking for some time; and was speaking regularly with the (new) employer.

Essentially, we feel "burned" for not being paid....even a portion for the candidate lasting only 3 weeks, and the fact that they "stiffed" us by going behind our backs to find someone themselves; and now they're coming back for another person to replace the four month candidate.

We've said that if we're to get involved again, it would be ONLY on the provision that this is a NEW order, (not a replacement as it is over 3 months) AND any guarantee is based on competency, and not on tenure, because they REALLY are paying too low salary, the working conditions MAY not be the greatest, and some candidates have problems with the Hiring Manager.

We also reminded them that once they decided NOT to pay; any and ALL guarantees are null and void, whether written or implied.

Are we being overly cautious? There's nothing to say they'll promise to pay, we'll find another candidate, and then they'll "say" that it's to replace the other.

The said they wanted at least a 3 month guarantee. They were willing to come down from 6 months. BUT, they wanted NO restrictions. In return, they'll agree to pay the full amount, and if the person DOESN'T work out, to ask for a replacement only; not the money back as THEY demanded and didn't pay earlier.

But if the work environment and Manager are bad, aren't we just setting ourselves up for more punishment and potential nonpayment?

AccordingToDanny replies:

Let me be practical with you, because this is fraught with emotion.

- You feel "stiffed because they didn't pay.
- Rest assured they feel outraged that your candidates last just a few weeks.
- You feel it's absurd to be tagged with culpability. The candidates started work. Your job ended. It's the company's fault if working conditions don't keep people happy.
- They believe these candidates were never sincere, or worse, that you knew and didn't tell them.

What we don't understand, we can make mean anything.

None of these emotions is useful. So let's dial it down and get real.

- If the client is poorly perceived by the marketplace, has little or no attractive elements, and refuses to change the compensation, you should cut your losses and end the relationship. In my experience, they do not change their culture for one search firm. Move on.

- If you decide to work with them, you must do a better job of collections. Verify the placement and ask who is in charge of processing the invoice, call that person and introduce yourself, and be specific and insistent that they will lose the hard negotiated guarantee if not paid on time. Verify in email. Then you have a record you can refer to.

But as far as the "no restrictions" stance or their posturing...don't get crazy. As you predict, should another situation happen where a candidate lasts, say 81 days on a 90 day guarantee...or the candidate tells your client they are not happy or are looking, your client is not going to pay. They are going to hold that check regardless of the guarantee, and they are smart to do so, because headhunters hate to sue for money.

If you decide not walk away, and I really wish you would, you need to qualify to the fullest every candidate that goes in, and cover resignation, counteroffer, and other interviews pending, for every candidate that accepts. Make it a policy not to allow a candidate to accept without giving you contact info on the jobs they were applying or interviewing for. Get these leads. Fill those jobs, and your candidate will make the new home you've put them in stick...good luck.

He Wants Out... I Am Working on More for the Company

Dear Danny:

I placed a high level candidate as head of business development with a company 9 months ago. This candidate has knocked the cover off the ball by adding key staff, energizing the organization and attaining the annual production goals by the end of the first half. The problem is that his manager, the president and owner of the company, is unpredictable and a terrible leader and motivator. While my candidate has been wildly successful there, he is unhappy with the owner and is considering moving. He has already approached me to discuss his dilemma. I would never pull a placed candidate out of a company, but this candidate called me. Also, based on his feedback and comments of others within this organization, this owner treats his people very poorly. Should I work again with this candidate? Should I have a frank conversation with this owner (with whom I have a good working relationship) but which might expose this candidate?

Just to add more ambiguity to the discussion, I am working on several other positions for this company which would report to another senior executive that I understand is also unhappy and considering a move. I don't want to put any more candidates into a potentially bad career situation. Any thoughts would be appreciated.

AccordingToDanny replies:

You really have three problems.

First, it is OK to work with the person you placed and who has asked you for help in getting out. He called you. That is the NAPS rule. But let's not stop with this declarative

85

statement. I could send you to the Ask Danny library with a link, but I'd rather share the full text with you here of what I wrote to another recruiter who had a similar question because it is not just a question of the NAPS rule.

I wrote:

Tonight, at some point, you will go to sleep with yourself. You need to feel good about that. I see that as priority number one, and while it's tempting to get on my ethical soapbox and remind you of Karma, truth, justice and the American way, let's examine this a little.

... what is the actual ethical standard? It's not what some think. Some maintain that all clients, and to them that includes everyone who ever sent you a check, are off limits. For all candidates. Forever.

Here's the actual standard, which you can verify through NAPS. You can work with anyone who calls you! That's right. As long as you did not solicit them and they called you, you can work with them with a completely clear conscience. This appears to be the case in the example you cite.

Now, about sleeping tonight. You could easily have manipulated this situation by 1) asking for a referral of someone "just like you", 2) you could have asked casually if they were "okay" because they didn't sound like themselves.

If you did so, you know in your heart it was your intention to solicit them. And that is wrong, and, as Mark Twain said, "Always do what's right, this will gratify some and astonish the rest."

But if they came to you of their own volition, and they are ready to move and you know they're placeable, you'd be foolish not to work with them. And you can do so without guilt or fear of reprisal.

The only caveat I would throw in is that in my office, because we are geared toward retainers, we won't work with anyone from any of our retained accounts regardless of how they came to us. This is a business judgment on my part to help sell retainers. It is protection money; it has nothing to do with ethics.

So ask yourself the hard question and then act. Sleep well.

Now to the second problem, you say the company owner treats his people poorly. You say he is a terrible leader and motivator and unpredictable – the reason your candidate wants to leave. And... you are working on several other searches for this owner and you are now afraid that you could be sending more people to a bad career situation, **and** you "understand" that the another senior executive is unhappy and considering a move **and** he is the hiring authority for the positions you are now recruiting for. This all adds up to one big mare's nest. You ask if you should talk to the owner.

My question is this – to accomplish what? Retain the person you placed? Retain the other senior executive? Salve your fears that you are not sending others to career doom? What do you think you could say that would save these situations?

Telling this person that you are hearing on the street that he has a bum reputation is not going to get this person to change. Can you imagine his responding to your call this way? "Funny you should say that, I was telling my wife only this morning that I am a terrible leader and motivator, and unpredictable." I think I will change?" Don't make the call.

What would I recommend one of my recruiters do with this set of circumstances?

First, work with the candidate you placed as he is asking you to help him make a move. Second, don't play business

psychologist. Third, consider cutting your losses and not
working on the other searches.

FOR OWNERS AND MANAGERS

"The sad, perennial refrain of the owner/manager: Why is it the talented ones make no effort and the one who try have no talent."

Hiring Experienced Recruiters	p. 91
My Top Performer Now Works "Union Rules"	p. 95
Good... but Not Enough Activity	p. 98
Intensive Care for Recruiters	p.100
I Want to Expand – But Not Open More Offices	p.102
Call Accounting and Call Volume	p.106
He Has Asked to Go Straight Commission	p.108
Bringing In a GM	p.110
Trouble with Mom	p.113

Hiring Experienced Recruiters

Dear Danny:

Our executive search business is finally starting to come back in some of our niches. I have tried to hire experienced recruiters on the theory that there should be a lot of experienced recruiters out of work or stuck in the niches that have NOT started to come back (like IT).

I have not figured out how to find & screen good experienced recruiters.

I have advertised and Web posted. I hired 5 experienced recruiters over 6 months. One was great, but 4 in a row turned out to be worthless.

Where can I find experienced recruiters? How can I tell if they are worthless or good when I screen them? Should I just give up on hiring experienced recruiters & go back to training people with no recruiting experience like we did in 2000? Training inexperienced people was very much hit-and-miss and took a lot of time and money, and many were only marginal.

AccordingToDanny replies:

I sense your frustration, and it makes sense to tackle this now, because as the market improves, you'll be buried in work, but won't be able to capitalize on it without more staff. (Hmmm, sounds like you're feeling your clients' pain...keep that in mind when you negotiate with them.)

It might be helpful to discuss the merits of Experienced Recruiters versus Newbies!

PROS of Experienced Recruiters:

1) No initial downtime training. (Okay, some, but not as much.)
2) They will bring a potential book of business they can tap into immediately.
3) In a good market, they should reach strong levels with little maintenance.
4) You shouldn't have to drive them; motivation should be built-in and assumed.

CONS of Experienced Recruiters:

1) Generally, they have not just come off the greatest year ever.
2) They want to do it "their" way.
3) They have no loyalty to you. (If loyalty were big for them, you wouldn't have them.)
4) When things get tough, they run.
5) They want higher bases, higher commission rates.
6) Hey, what happened to their book of business?
7) Their call level is low to moderate, and it's hard as hell to get them to change.

Now, let's look at Newbies.

PROS of Newbies:

1) Lots of energy and curiosity. The proverbial blissful ignorance.
2) Through high call levels, they'll fall into things.
3) They're hungrier.
4) They don't think they know everything.
5) You can form the mutual bond of loyalty that tenure is based on.
6) They don't cost as much.
7) When they make a placement, they're not all "hey, it's what I do", they're HAPPY!!

CONS of Newbies:

1) They don't even know what they don't know.
2) You tell them a million times and they still don't get it.
3) You think you were so much better and smarter when you started. (You're embellishing.)
4) They require tons of training and attention, especially in the first few weeks.
5) They might be really good and leave because it's too hard.
6) They might be really bad and they stay because it's too hard for you to fire people.

The deciding factors for you have to be:

1) Your ability and desire to train. (If you don't train them they have no chance. Zero.)
2) Your culture.
3) The market.

The first two are personal and you need to be the judge. To me the market is the wild card. Newbies will require less attention in a great market. If you get them up and running they will be there 3-5 years from now, seasoned, successful, *and* full of themselves. (The last comes with the territory.) If you are niched and have the work for them to come in and recruit on, and can get them the confidence that comes with early success and $$, I would always prefer newbies.

But if your personal makeup means you can't stand babysitting, and want to make things happen faster, go the experienced route. But even with experienced recruiters, you must 1) establish policies and procedures (especially regarding fees and terms of guarantees), and 2) provide an orientation/training of at least a day or two, *in conjunction* with getting them specific AccordingToDanny training. Many an experienced recruiter's skills have often eroded, and no one calls them on it. The ATD-based training is a graceful way for them to plagiarize.

Now, where to get them?

I covered this in my Webinar available on www.accordingtodanny.com – *Where Do Recruiters Cone From?* But until you look at it, think about this...

You have no hotter job to fill than the one on your staff. When you have a hot job, what do you do?

1) Ask your normal contacts for referrals.
2) Get the word out to your network.
3) Post on the Internet and/or advertise.
4) Recruit.

Most owners only do #3....that ought to tell you something...we get specific in the Webinar.

My Top Performer Now Works "Union Rules"

Dear Danny:

A bit of background: I have been owner for just over a year, recruited into recruiting by a recruiter who wondered why I shouldn't be recruiting rather than staying in the industry I had been in for 20+ years. I enjoy the work and am committed to building a strong organization.

Right now I have one experienced AE (with me almost from the beginning) and two AEs who are real newbies. The experienced AE started off strong — $200K in billings the first six months. She is now seemingly plateauing. Every index of her performance is off — hours worked, hours on the phone, calls made. And so her job order and send out numbers are down. She seems satisfied with her income to date and has started to work what I'd like to call "union rules" — coming in at the official start time, going home promptly at 5 p.m. She used to work long hours, work at home.

I worry about two things: 1) how do I get the person who has been my best performer to get back on track, and 2) how do I not let a "union rules" atmosphere pervade my office. To build my organization, I know that it can't just be me hitting the numbers — number of calls, hours on the phone, number of job orders and send outs, etc. And my best performer is becoming a bad example.

Now, I don't want to lose this best performer. Having her walk because I come down too hard is not something I want to have happen. I also know that I have to set a standard for performance for the new people, the ones I have now and the ones I will hire, a rule like you have of no placements in three months = time for them to get a new job.

95

So, what can I do to motivate my best performer to get back on track? It seems to me that this is the first thing I have to do. Am I right? If not, where should I start? What should I do?

AccordingToDanny replies:

Because you are a new owner/manager, I want you to take my answer in the spirit in which it is intended, because it is people like you that AccordingToDanny was intended for; so that you could, with the help of our tools, save yourself from a world of hurt, and ultimately become very successful.

You have found yourself in one of our industry's biggest traps. Most owners I talk to lack the character and foresight to do the right thing. I hope you're different. I hope you can hear this. Here goes:

You can't have it both ways. You can't say you don't want the "union rules" sloppiness and then tell me you don't want to lean on her so hard you lose her. Here's what happens 90% of the time: you create an environment where you do not practice what you preach, everyone knows it, and so they start working half heartedly because she is and you haven't let her go, and you end up with a sloppy system that is nearly impossible to unravel and a culture of mediocrity. Why? For her? Let me clue you in on something. If she started strong, had success, and then began the slow, inexorable march out the door by reducing her intensity, activity and effort:

She's leaving!!

It's over. She may not have found another job yet (though often they have), and she might not even be fully aware of it yet. But superstars in our business, whether they start slowly or successfully, **fall in love with the business. Their**

intensity is soaring at the first year's end. They have found a home. What you have on your hands is a person who found she can do the business but doesn't want to, and it is merely a matter of time before she decides she is wasting her and your time.

Know what else? The owner is nearly always the last to know. She is probably telling other folks in the office, and they are keeping her secret and you are being pitied, and that is unacceptable and pathetic for an owner.

You need to find the strength to go the other way. Your culture of discipline and excellence is more important than any one person's production. You let her and everyone else know the standards. You tell her it's time to end the sophomore slump and get some billings or get out. You offer to help. Buy an hour's teleconference with me. I will assess her skills, see what her mechanics are, and pump her up. But make her play ball!! Your way.

And then if she doesn't respond, take a deep breath and let her go.

It will be scary and it will hurt at first. And then you will realize:

- the world didn't end
- you got respect from the folks who remain
- the man in the mirror looks happy and proud.

The French have a saying, "the graveyards are filled with indispensable men."

Set this precedent now. It will pay off for years to come. I promise.

Good... But Not Enough Activity

Dear Danny:

What do I do with a consultant who is proving to be excellent in all ways but seems to have a bit of a problem with either perfectionism or possibly cold-calling/referring? Everything this guy does is great but he does not manage to get enough activity to meet his goals. I am particularly talking about candidates. We need a certain number per week to have both good sendouts and the throwaways that sometimes end up as placements. I do not know how to get him to meet the standard instead of hitting 1/3 to 1/2 of it. I should note that with these numbers he will still hit about $220k or so...

AccordingToDanny replies:

Hats off for caring enough to push a $220K consultant. Most owners feel they have bigger problems and gravitate toward the proverbial "squeaking wheel." But you're right to be concerned. The problem you have identified is a big one, one that often prevents a $220K biller from ever achieving the upper echelon of recruiting.

Why, because they are combining their *ultra selectivity* (AKA, the playing God syndrome) with a given energy level.

So, formula wise, if G/E = the energy level required to make the calls and generate the activity to hit $220K.

And T = time...and U/S = their ultra selectivity... then $G/E \times U/S \times T$ = their capacity as a recruiter.

Right now they are getting positive reinforcement because they're closing some deals with this formula. But in time, and I'm assuming this is a relatively new recruiter, the following is axiomatic... their

1) G/E will go down (call level, intensity, etc.)
2) U/S will get worse or stay the same as they get more niched.

This spells disaster. The market is so robust and growing that just when the top producing recruiter is being less selective (because their clients are less choosy), your recruiter will miss the boat or get beat out by more aggressive "when in doubt, send them out" types.

I'm not saying your recruiter needs to abandon good qualifying, but they need to move closer to center and increase their activity now, so that when the inevitable, inexorably slow but unstoppable slowdown in their G/E comes, they're coming down from a higher level, and their expertise carries the day.

Having said that, you're fighting one of the toughest battles. To tell your recruiter this makes you appear ungrateful, difficult to please, and hypercritical. Only one thing, in my experience, teaches them this critical lesson:

When a client has to hires one of the candidates they had at their fingertips, but in their infinite wisdom, chose not to send!

If your recruiter can change without having to learn this bitter, bitter lesson, he/she will be extraordinary.

Intensive Care for Recruiters

Dear Danny:

I've heard about your ICU program for recruiters needing your intensive care. This is my question:

What are the elements of an ICU program? I need to develop my own program and would rather base what I do on what you do than try to figure it out from scratch.

AccordingToDanny replies:

ICU, like getting old, is not for wimps!

It requires tremendous patience and focus on the part of both you and your recruiter. You have to really believe your recruiter is worth this increased amount of attention for a short period, and they have to want the help. Anyone who is faking it will render it useless.

It's generally a month in duration. The first week I observe. Literally, I sit at their desk ALL DAY! I listen to their calls and watch how they organize and move around their desk. I write down everything. I ask very few questions the first week, but I take a ton of notes.

It's amazing what you'll learn. Somebody comes up with recruiter Ritalin and they will get filthy rich!

End of week one, going into the weekend, I deliver my findings and we make a deal. I usually concentrate on two or three major areas, and do not bite off more than I or they can chew. For example, right now I am working with one of my recruiters on 1) the way he writes jobs, and 2) his tendency to jump from one plan to another, never getting into a natural rhythm. Those are big changes.

In a new ICU program here is the deal:

- They must show me, and I must approve, their physical plan every day. It can be generated on the computer, but it has to be printed out.
- Their desk must be clean during calling hours. I check.
- They must stay off the Internet during the prime calling hours.
- I set send out and job order goals for each week, and check them at the end of every day.
- They tape all closing calls.
- We role play their marketing and recruiting scripts.
- They take no time off during ICU.
- They don't argue. We tried it their way, damn it, let's try it mine.

They hate me for a while. Then it works. And they like me again. Funny how that is!

I Want to Expand – But Not Open More Offices

Dear Danny:

I run a successful Finance and Accounting search firm in a major state with a lot of population centers. I was trained by one of the name brand F/A recruiting firms so I run it now on the local market/face-to-face interview model. I want to expand my operation to other parts of the state, but I do not want to open local offices. My thought is to add staff in my office here to do local recruiting in specific territories in other parts of the state, i.e. have a team who recruits for Greater X, another team for Greater Y, etc.

I am comfortable giving up the face-to-face. Where I need some guidance:

a) How smart is distance recruiting in delimited territories?
b) Is there anything special I need to do in my job order and recruiting to adjust for the fact there will be no client visits or face-to-face interviewing?
c) Do you know of anyone how works on this model in F/A?

AccordingToDanny replies:

One of the traits of successful people that I have uncovered in my time of mentoring some of the best people in the industry is this:

They are unafraid to tinker.

Even with their clothes, image, niche, industry, comp structure, or even some of the sacred cows of the placement

102

process. This often yields spectacular failures, and they are always better for having tried it. Often it is the second incarnation of whatever they are trying to change that produces the transformational success they seek, but you never get to second base without taking your foot off the first base bag.

So now let's talk. It's a great idea to eschew other local offices. The world has changed. You don't need other lease space to grow. Some folks go with virtual recruiters working out of their house. But I chose your way. I understood companies were not paying for face-to-face interviews, they were paying for the access to talented people who can do Monday what the guy who left Friday was doing **with no training.**

Further, I learned that I could evaluate candidates nearly as well on the phone as I could in person. By using our process of structured interviewing, by knowing our job order down pat, and by asking qualifying questions, there was very little lost by recruiting outside of my local territory, but so much gained:

- It obviously increases the number of jobs you can find to fill.
- By having a team work, say, greater Y, they become known in that market and the database and referral quotients rise quickly.
- You can then cross-sell the entire state. (Set up a fair split system for each unit.)
- The reduced number of client visits and interviews increases phone and production time.

What do you need to do differently?

There are two areas of concern. You must reference check your candidates before sending them out, and in that reference check you must say, and the wording is essential so

103

you avoid breaking EEOC discrimination laws, *"Since I will not be able to meet ___ personally, tell me about his/her presentation skills."* This will give you a physical description of the person, the one thing you can't get through qualifying on the telephone. Remember, the world is shallow, and set up for attractive people, you need a way in your new model to get at the stars. In your interviewing you must work harder to get at the underlying motive, or "pain" that a candidate is feeling. You won't be able to look them in the eye anymore to determine their veracity, you get it from asking:

- Why move now?
- What's driving this?
- Where else have you posted, or interviewed? What efforts have you made to move? (No effort = Not Serious.)
- Will you move for a lateral or a small increase? (If it's just for money, you'll lose them to fear of change or counteroffer).

There's no real need to change your job order, though I would recommend you see our Webcast on job orders - *Job Opportunities, Not Job Orders.* We have revamped how we take them and since the model I follow, and have for over a decade, is the very one you are envisioning, I think it might be helpful. We have not interviewed candidates, face-to-face, for years, and our volume of business more than tripled within 18 months of freeing us up. You instinct is right on here. You're contemplating the right thing. We went national with the approach, and niched ourselves in sales, but F/A one state is a good start. You'll get all the same benefits. A bonus is you'll find yourself getting higher level jobs with bigger fees.

My model has been emulated by a number of firms who specialize in F/A, and due to the functional nature of the positions, as with engineers, it is even more effective. With the salespeople I place, there is a bigger weight placed on style, image and dress. And yet the model has worked well for us. I'm sure it will for you.

As a person trained in a major name brand organization, that tells me you're used to structure and numbers keeping. Have all your new folks track their numbers on my site if that would help. But whichever way you choose, make this move. It's a great way to expand in a good market and keep your expenses down. Great idea!

Call Accounting and Call Volume

Dear Danny:

We are in the process of buying a call accounting package to monitor our calls. What are your requirements for phone time and amount of calls a consultant should make each day? Thanks.

AccordingToDanny replies:

Ahh, numbers. Recruiters, when in their cups, are fond of saying, or rather slurring, that the business is fundamentally unstable. Feast and famine. Up and down.

But they're wrong. Or rather, to be kind, they are uneducated as to the magnificent magic of mathematics. If you hit the right numbers, track them assiduously, and most important of all, never try to outsmart them or think you've outgrown them, you can predict almost to the penny how much you'll earn year to year, and you can do so without the prosperity-panic syndrome that makes up the life of most recruiters.

So here are the numbers:

Call accounting wise. You want 4 hours a day on the phone. Rookies will hit more in their first few months, senior people will have days when they are working very hard and come in less. Anyone who has less than 2.5 hours per day is fooling themselves and will pay a price.

The volume of calls depends on niche. But 75-100 attempts a day as a combination of all calls is a reasonable number. Remember that this should be balanced in a "pipeline" approach, so that we are always marketing, even when we have jobs, and always making some candidate acquisition calls, even when we need jobs. That way the pipeline stays full, the recruiter avoids burn out...

Not that there's anything wrong with burn out. If you burn out, that means at least for a while, you were on fire!

He Has Asked To Go Straight Commission

Dear Danny:

One of my account executives recently asked me about going on straight commission. He averages about $215k in cash in and he has been with us about 3.5 years. This was the first AE I hired and I brought him in at a high compensation agreement. He is paid $30,000, with a $5000 monthly quota and commissions of 45% for the first $100k cash in, 50% for the 2nd $100k cash in and 55% for cash in over $200k cash in. This is a pretty rich comp plan and I'm not sure if I can do a lot better with a commission only plan. Any suggestions you have on a good commission only plan?

AccordingToDanny replies:

Hey Money Bags, settle down!! I'm afraid to post this on the Web for fear of my people calling you for a job!!

You're right that your plan is already generous. But this AE is taking some of your risk away and is easing cash flow by going straight commish - no big deal when producing, potentially critically important during slumps...

Go to 50% sooner. From $0-100K. That's the easy part. They get more, earlier for taking the risk.

The problem is that 52.5% and 55% are not challenging enough. You're paying Pinnacle level rates for average billing. Show him/her this if it helps. Go 52.5% at $100K, but keep it there until $300K; then go to 55%, and even 57.5% above $400K, and 60% above $500K. Leave it there, hot shot!!

The other thing I would recommend is a kicker at year end. A $10K bonus if you hit $500K in billing is one I have used. A company car at some astronomical level - a "Tercel at two hundred" - is nice alliteration but not in the spirit of the thing!

Before you do any of these, make sure you know the motive. Is it to justify more money? Great. Is it to test the waters to see if they can live without a base or draw? Are they unhappy? A straight commission plan under these circumstances is a move toward the door.

And I'll add this: most AE's crumble under the pressure of straight commission. They qualify less, fold faster in negotiations. However toking the draw, its symbolism and allusion of security often helps them. Sometimes they don't even know how much until they are straight commission. So if you do this, watch closely. It may not be worth it.

Bringing in a GM

Dear Danny:

I am strongly considering bringing an individual into my business and need ideas for compensation. I reviewed your posted plans and none fit this scenario. I will be stepping out of the active management of my firm but will still do some recruiting and marketing. That aside, I am talking with a senior person who manages a franchise office (there are no non-compete issues) about coming to our firm and managing it for some salary and profit-sharing based upon production of recruiters as well as his own. He will also bring a few employees to our firm and renew our non-legal search arm. He wants some potential ownership interest, which I am open to if production is there. Have you seen or do you have any sample plans covering this? Thanks for any ideas and help!

AccordingToDanny replies:

After 10 years of building my firm, I had to tackle this very delicate issue myself. I wanted to continue to produce in a rainmaking capacity, and to grow my firm, then 12 recruiters, now double that, but I needed to get out of the day-to-day: check planners, fix the copier, settle petty disputes, etc...

I hired a general manager, who happened to be one of my most loyal and gifted recruiters, but I did so after surveying many of the large firms in the industry who had made this "growing pains" jump. All were privately-held firms, where the owner was the prime recruiter and kingpin, but wanted an exit strategy. Here are the rules as I looked over their compensation landscape....

110

- GMs should have the ability to make 5-10% of the office's cash-in bonus or commission.
- This schedule should not kick in until the office surpasses its "break even" point.
- The GM should be paid slightly more on the production of new people than on that of experienced people.
- They must also be producers, so the 5-10% should be based on a graduated plan tied to their billings.

For example, you might say you would pay a GM 5% of the house cash in, but that they would get 6% of cash in for the balance of the fiscal year as long as they surpass 200K in personal billings. And so on up to 10%!

Here's the thing you have to decide. Do you want a billing manager? Or a partner who grows your firm? Above 10-15 people, something has to give. They either will ignore the newbies and growth because your comp plan ties them to production, or you can go the other way, and say you WON'T pay them on anything more than 200K, so that any billings they do after that they simply get their House % of 5-10%. This incents them to produce enough to stay active and credible, but makes them see the big picture is other recruiters and growth. This is what I do here with my general manager.

Partnership should be off the table for 3 three years. Set production and staffing goals and commit to making them partners if they hit those goals. Don't be stingy. Make it 10/15% of the firm, and if you want an exit strategy, begin a vesting schedule where they can opt to buy you out over time.

Search firms are not very marketable to other buyers, but when you sell to employees, you maintain your legacy, and you retain control.

Lastly, keep the base moderate. Make them hungry. Normally you see base salaries in the $35-100K range depending on the area of the country and the size of the search firm. So if someone got a $100K base, and 5% of the gross, and was paid 33% on their personal production of 200K, and the office did $4 million dollars....their income would be $366K, or about 9% of the house. That's a very fair package in contemporary search firms.

Good luck, it's a big decision. Make sure you care about this person. This is not strictly a business decision. I would take a bullet for any of the 8 partners in my firm. For my GM, I would take two.

Trouble with Mom

Dear Danny:

I am not even sure where to start. In 1994, I came to work as a recruiter in the family business for my mom. The office was out of her home and it was an ideal situation. My mom has been in the recruiting industry within her niche for almost 30 years. I did a lot of changing of the business. Enough so that I worked my way into a 50/50 partnership with her.

 Business was BOOMING!! We moved the business out of her house and into an office and hired on recruiters and support staff.   All along she has told me that this was great, but I suspect otherwise. Since I automated the office, all she can do is play FreeCell and Solitaire on the computer. She has worked her way into 1,908 FreeCell games and 1,963 Solitaire games since 11/03. She has become the single most de-motivating factor in this company and I am resentful. I have told her about these resentments. I have told her that she needs to go home when she begins that obnoxious clicking sound and I remind her that these same games on the computer here are also on her computer at home.

I don't know what else I can do. I have tried everything:

1) I stopped working myself and did what she did...th at only got me into financial troubles by spending money on eBay.

2) I flat out told her that this company is going to hell in a hand basket and she agreed that she needs to work more. That only got me a day and a half's worth of work.

3)I have removed the games only to find them on her computer again.

4) I have thought of moving to a different desk in the office, but I thing that only puts a band aid on the problem.

113

5) I have tried to put her in a figurehead kind of position by sending her to industry stuff so that she can schmooze. I have tried to get her to train the new recruiters. When she works, she is AMAZING, one of the best I have ever seen, but I am lucky if she works 1 hour a day. She is here everyday, but I would be happier if she just wasn't here.

I have done everything to be respectful of her and I am tired of the pleasantries. I know that I got into the family business out of my own free will. I understand that family businesses are difficult...believe me I KNOW!!

All I want now is to get nasty with her and tell her to retire already and GET OUT, but I suspect that will not only hurt the business, but also our relationship as Mother/Daughter. Any ideas of how to get a business partner to retire? I need help.

AccordingToDanny replies:

I knew all I had to know when I read that you counted the precise number of games of FreeCell (1908) and Solitaire (1963) you mom has played on her computer. This is not minor stress, this is eating at you, and if you do not take some action, you will resent only one person more than your Mom, and that is yourself, for allowing it to happen.

Let's first pay our respects. What I am going to suggest doesn't mean that I don't understand:

1) All moms are sacred. We owe them our life, (but not our lives).
2) She taught you the business.
3) Long after this is decided, she's your Mom.
4) Those damn games are addictive!!
5) I know you don't want to hurt her.

Having said that, this chick is toast!

She has got to go. The fact that she can be effective one hour a day on those days when the computer is down notwithstanding, she has peaked, she is in decline, and she will take you down. Smiling all the way. And when it's over, she'll blame you for not being as good as she was, and not being a tougher business person. You must not let that day come.

You tried some excellent conventional strategies, but she's too far gone. She's not feeling any pain. Oh, she may get a twinge of remorse when you do the guilt trip thing, but halfway through your speech, her mouse finger is twitching and she's thinking she can break her personal record.

Here's what I would do.

Phase One: I would sit her down and tell her you feel the biz is going south and you have decided to look for a job. You will run the biz in good faith until you find something, but it's your intention to get away from the stress and work for someone else. She'll think it's a bluff. So leave postings near her desk, call the weather report and lower your voice when she comes near. On those days, dress real well and leave early. (Go home and make calls, don't let your biz suffer.) When she asks where you're going, say, "you don't want to know." Give her a list of things to do while you're gone. Give her some of the Mom treatment. "It's time you learn to take care of yourself; I'll be gone soon."

Phase Two: I would get a lawyer to draw up a dissolution agreement (if you have a corporation) outlining how the company goes out of existence. If you know a lawyer well enough, tell him you want the agreement in case you need it, but you also want to scare your Mom straight, and let him conduct a real, professional and scary as hell meeting.

Phase Three (concurrent): You should not only ignore her, I would buy her a new computer with higher tech games as a "parting gift" because you feel so bad about leaving her. But you must act as if you have moved on. This will freak her out.

All of this, if planned correctly, should take 3 weeks. She will at some point sit you down and say "what will happen to me?" Find the Clark Gable courage to say, "Frankly, Ma, I don't give a damn."

End the meeting. Wait a day or at least overnight. Then go to her and tell her that you have an alternative: Retirement. Now. Out of the Office. DON'T BELIEVE HER WHEN SHE SAYS SHE'LL CHANGE.

When she agrees, throw her the sweetest retirement party ever. She deserves it. You'll feel the resentment dissipate. You'll live longer. So will she.

RECRUITING

Best Recruiting Call Ever – Steve Jobs to the President of Pepsi: "Do you want to make sugar water your whole life, or do you want to make a difference?"

What Can I Say about His Termination?   p.119
Non-competes   p.121
He Looks Like a Job Hopper   p.124
But... Tell Me about My Competition for the Job?   p.126
Do I Have to Cold Call Recruit?   p.128
Covering the Candidate   p.131

117

What Can I Say About His Termination?

Dear Danny:

A candidate was terminated from his previous employer due to a company vehicle accident and tested positive for marijuana which is in violation of company policy and cause for termination. I contacted his supervisor and he gave the candidate an outstanding reference and would definitely rehire if company policy would permit him to. How much can or should I disclose to a potential client regarding his termination? The candidate's expertise in the oilfield makes him a placeable candidate.

AccordingToDanny replies:

Compassion is a funny thing. It is easiest to access when you feel you are making an active choice to exercise it. When you discover something someone was trying to keep from you, the road to forgiveness and understanding becomes undulating and difficult to traverse.

The art required here is to give, with all apologies to Fox News, a fair and balanced reference. You must point out.

1) The candidate was upfront with this info. He/she wants you to know.
2) They own their own mistake. They have taken accountability for it.
3) (If true,) other references have shown no pattern, and this is a first-time offense.
4) His direct supervisor gave an excellent reference and implied the company's very strict policy is the only thing keeping him/her from rehiring this candidate.

Now you remind the client they have two choices. But tell them first that so much of this depends on the client's frame

119

of reference. (You never say in your question if they were under the influence when the vehicle accident occurred.) If the client has never had a day of fun in their whole life and sees a recreational drug like marijuana as evil incarnate, then we should not waste anyone's time.

But if the client, like me, like you perhaps, has a foible or two of their own, if they accept T.S. Eliot's premise that "human beings can only bear so much reality," then perhaps we can do this candidate the compassionate favor of not allowing one bad decision to adversely affect their whole life.

Then suggest they see the candidate, in strong terms, with an open ended alternative date close.

So you must make a decision. Pass on working with the candidate, or, if you believe in them, get behind them and make a case.

Non-competes

Dear Danny:

Increasingly, we're running up against non-competes as issues in recurring and attracting currently employed top-performers from one company to another. Beyond the "I'm not an attorney, so I can't give you legal advice," what are your suggestions on how and when to address non-competes to minimize their potentially negative impact on closing a deal? Thanks.

AccordingToDanny replies:

There's a great scene in "The Untouchables" where Sean Connery asks Kevin Costner what he is prepared to do to stop Al Capone. And Costner's line is: "Everything under the law." To which Connery replies, "And *then* what are you prepared to do?"

Non-competes start, not with your candidates, as most recruiters see the problem, but with your clients in the taking of a job order. It must become part of your job order qualifying to say, in effect, that top players have non-competes, and companies are going to try to enforce them, and because this is not 2002, and these top performers are not desperate, or even needy, they will expect you to defend them from the non-compete, which means paying all the legal costs. And *then* what are you prepared to do? (To put this in context for you, it will generally cost a company between$10-40K to fight a non-compete. In our world, since I know your niche, this is a fraction of the revenue my candidates will bring in year after year. It's a no-brainer of an investment, and it builds loyalty in a way nothing else you do for this candidate ever will. It's the corporate equivalent of punching the school bully for your little brother. Or so I'm told. (My big brother let me get repeatedly pummeled.)

Pull this off and you can sell this as sizzle to your candidates, instead of living in fear of it.

Now the candidate side. This should be covered in the initial candidate qualifying, just after you have uncovered their pain, the true source of their wanting to make a move. Once you have established this you say:

"Let me be clear about something. All good people leave money on the table. Sometimes in the form of bonuses. Sometimes they spend money by walking out on a non-compete. Obviously we will try to negotiate a good faith release with your current company, but if it fails, then what are you prepared to do?"

I ask to see the non-compete. And I do look for reasonableness, both in scope and duration. If both are present, *I never tell them it won't hold up, that judges frown on these things.* Because it's not true. While some states, (like California) are "right to work" states and don't allow noncompetes, they allow trade secrets and confidentiality agreements, which amount to the same thing, and they hold up quite well.

I go the other way. I tell them they all hold up in some fashion. They may get an injunction or they may get a percentage of your income or they may just make you stay away from two key clients or throw out four pages but keep three. The point is even if it's just the hassle factor, they waste your time, and they cost money to defend.

So now what? You are an indentured servant? You stay miserable? They own you? Is that any way to live? Get them mad. Fighting mad!

I point out:

Go to your boss. (Once you have my offer.) Tell him your problem. You want to work this out, but you want to work.

Can't we, to borrow from Brother Rodney, all just get along? This is the "it's a big world out there" approach and it works well. Get a release and we're home free.

But if it doesn't go well, tell him it's your intention to move on, and you'll attempt to respect the non-compete, but you will do what's best for your family, and eventually, you'll be in the industry. This is, after all, America.

If I have managed both sides well, I wait until I'm far enough into the process to decide which way I go, which side I squeeze. But don't leave it up to lawyers. Make it happen...

He Looks Like a Job Hopper

Dear Danny:

I am working with a very successful candidate who has worked for several insurance companies which have closed — making his resume look like he's a job hopper! He works a very small niche and the employers should be aware of the closings (most are). I've tried the standard methods of overcoming the objection of "too many jobs in a short period of time" — do you have any suggestions?

AccordingToDanny replies:

Please don't ask me how I know this.

But it is amazing to me how a guy who, at 40, never having been married, never having been engaged, is perceived by women to be less attractive than a guy, (I'm thinking of friends of mine you understand), who has been married a few times, and is a proven failure in the world of relationships. Why wouldn't he be considered damaged goods? Why wouldn't they prefer the person who just "never found the right woman," but is now ready to really commit?

I'll tell you why. If they've been married before, then you know...

1) They have been vetted sexually.
2) They have some redeeming qualities and references to prove it — read the divorce decrees.
3) They are relentlessly optimistic about love and life.
4) They have a sense of humor.

So here's the deal. You need to re-direct your company's concern by using this analogy.

They should not be concerned about why he/she made a couple of bad choices. They are not professional job changers. They are successful at their job, with a track record to prove it. The question is not why they made the changes, but what did the companies that kept hiring them see in them to convince them they were not damaged goods, but, instead, someone who had seen the light and now know what they want? They have been vetted. Don't measure them on their judgment; measure them on performance. Make your clients romantic and wistful.

If that doesn't work, sell the negative.

"My candidate is flawed, no doubt. He/she is a tremendous insurance executive with a great track record of performance, but he/she is a feckless optimist. Tell them that the department is going to be built around them, the funding is going to come through, and they're going to be the next VP, or just plain ask him/her to believe, and he/she is a sucker.

"But what you get with that flaw is a relentless optimist who refuses to quit, who goes down with the ship, and is blind to certain realities because he/she is committed. He/she is a life force who is fun to be around. Can I find you someone who has never made a move and therefore never made a mistake? Yeah, I could, but you wouldn't want them. They're retired; they just have not told anyone yet. They'll draw a paycheck for the next twenty years and haven't had an original idea in years. You ought to see my candidate because of his/her flaw, not in spite of it."

Good luck

But... Tell Me about My Competition for the Job?

Dear Danny:

How do you answer a candidate who asks you to give him/her an idea as to the competition, when you are providing all of the candidates?

AccordingToDanny replies:

My dad used to tell me to never ask for something I wasn't willing to give. Now that I think about it, it didn't keep me from asking him for things, but it still is excellent advice, and relevant to your question.

They are asking you for something they surely wouldn't want you to give others. Would they be comfortable with you telling other candidates that their competition is, for example 1) out of work and desperate, 2) used to work at Gartner Group as their New England Sales Manager but got crosswise with the boss, 3) is making $72K, recently divorced, and has a child with special learning needs? Where do they want you to draw the line? Are they really comfortable with you making this call on an arbitrary basis every time you get asked the question?

A wiser policy is confidentiality; impartially doled out to everyone you deal with. Client and candidate. Suffice it to say you have competition, and suffice it further to say some or all of that competition is keenly interested in the job, but you will not give out details of their situation, and you can rest assured they will never hear your details. It's the kind of policy that protects everyone, costs no one, and makes it easier for everyone involved to breathe.

Which brings me back to my dad, who also told me, in the queen mother of back handed compliments, "You shouldn't tell lies, Danny, you're not smart enough to keep it all straight."

And that's the truth.

Do I Have To Cold Call Recruit?

Dear Danny:

I have been recruiting for 10 years. I enjoy all the aspects of this business with the exception of cold calling for candidates. My business is geared toward 40k to 60K candidates. Quality and Engineering candidates working within Medical and Pharmaceutical companies. I have lost my patience speaking with operators who have no idea what I'm talking about and immediately put me in touch with the Director or VP of the department. My positions are of a lower level. Of course, when I talk to these Directors or VPs, I make this a multi-purpose call: 1) do they have any openings and 2) are they looking?

But my purpose was to recruit a lower level person. Consequently I have been relying on job boards to find candidates. I know you strongly advocate telephoning and I certainly agree with you. I need your help. Any suggestions?

AccordingToDanny replies:

Your question gave me pause, because my first reaction I don't think would serve you well. You and I are *wired* differently. One man's mendacity is another man's mental Mecca. You spoke in your question and in your subsequent conversation with my AccordingToDanny Operations Director about how much recruiting feels phony to you, circuitous, requiring way too much gamesmanship and telepathic tap dancing. It's not as black and white as a marketing call. You're not alone. I hear this a lot.

But it's not me. I **love** that part of it. When George Tenet recently resigned as Director of the CIA I truly expected a phone call about replacing him. I think I could get Bin Laden on the phone. I love not knowing who is going to answer and what I'm going to say. I love the labyrinth of questions, the battle of wits with secretaries and gatekeepers. I have a ventriloquist's range of tone and inflection, depending on what my instincts tell me the call requires. When the Hoovers of the world started listing names of employees, I felt a little like a train conductor who has gotten to the top of his game, is looking out at the dazzling, pastoral countryside, and then looks up and sees an airplane zooming over the tracks. You know you can't compete, but something is lost.

But that's me and I romanticize the business totally out of proportion to what it is to most people.

You need to be in less pain. So rather than try to get you to recommit to basics you find out of sync with your character, I'm going to tell you something I rarely say to recruiters. You need to work the internet.

But not the way you have been. Use the people on the Net as referral sources. Tell them, *"I don't want you, you're wrong (pick a reason), but you have the tech qualifications/are in the vertical/right logistics for what I need, **who do you respect enough to want to help?**"*

Find junior folks on the Web and ask them for their bosses or senior colleagues.

Find high level consulting firms, preferably one man shows who are semi retired guys taking assignments for short term cash. They know everyone at a variety of companies and have no compunction about referrals. Do this off Google.

Consider a service like Eliyon. This allows you to find the URL's and names of 20,000, 000 passive candidates. We have it in our office and so far are very impressed.

129

Get the references of everyone on the Web in your niche who lists them, and then call the references for indirect referrals for your jobs.

In short, surrender to your weakness. That could be the bravest move of all. You are not personally programmed for the "secret agentry" of cold recruiting. That's okay. You are fortunate enough to be in the biz at a time when this is no longer a fatal flaw. Recognize your hamartia, and embrace your strength.

And if all this fails, call me and we'll work a split. There's always a way.

Covering the Candidate

Dear Danny:

As a mostly contingency recruiter, I have always made a great effort to "cover the candidate," i.e., make sure to show a good candidate everything that is appropriate to show him.

Now that we are doing more retained work, I still would like to cover the candidate, but am not sure how appropriate that is to do on a retained search.

Your thoughts?

AccordingToDanny replies:

Covering the candidate is always the smartest way to ensure a placement. One of the ways we sometimes sell a retainer is with the "right of first refusal" clause. This clause simply states says that any candidate we RECRUIT for a client's retained search will not be sent to any other clients until the client decides not to pursue said candidate. If you have included such a clause in your contract, then obviously, you should not be sending your candidates elsewhere and breaching the contract. More often than not, we've not included the clause because it doesn't serve us well and we are able to get retainers without it. If a retained client asks us about whether or not we are sending the candidate elsewhere – we respond with an exuberant, "Of course" Sending the candidate elsewhere serves you Mr. Client in two ways. One, we are able to gauge a candidate's interest as it evolves and we know when exactly the interest grows serious by a candidate's disinterest in pursuing other things. Secondly, if we don't send him out, other recruiters will. In that case, the candidate is very unlikely to share with us the names of the competing opportunities, nor give us an ACCURATE picture of how they rank. If we know the competitive landscape we will be able to provide you the true picture of what competitive offers look like and we will know when the candidate is just trying to negotiate. As far as the candidate is concerned, we would rather not tell a candidate that we are just representing one company that pays us up front. We will increase our credibility in having the candidate's best interest at heart if we show them all the things they are qualified for and they choose whatever is best for them.

THE RERUITING LIFE

"The Life: Don't be afraid to burn out! Plan to burn out. If you burn out it means, at least for a while, you were on fire."

Doing Just Enough   p.135
Go for the Core   p.138
Reading for Rookies – Well... Not Just Rookies   p.140

Doing Just Enough

Dear Danny:

I am able to win business at will, able to show "grey men" (people cemented in their jobs) the light. However, I am bored. Why? Have you experienced boredom at any stage of your career? How can I motivate myself? Historically I used money as a motivator, but now have a home, cars, money family etc. and seem to be quite happy with my lot. At 29 I feel burnt out. I personally bill £300k working very lazily and manage my firm of 5 people. I need to start challenging myself and stop merely existing by DOING JUST ENOUGH. Can you help?

AccordingToDanny replies:

Do I get bored? I was yawning reading your question...

Top producers bore easily. Why? Because they're smart. They get "it." The business comes naturally to them. They're like the talented and gifted kids in fourth grade who never study because they can answer the questions and pass the tests just on their wits.

But hold on...what happens to those kids? They seldom are the ones with the PhD's or the outrageous success later in life. Because beyond a certain point talent, without discipline or drive isn't enough. The work gets harder, expectations greater...what do these kids do? Withdraw, become malcontents, and end up with detention notices in one pocket and a bag of pot in the other.

Not to be the Ghost of Christmas Future, but I have seen this often with top producers who first tell me they are bored. What they are really saying is they are afraid to commit to a bigger goal, a higher level of success, and they take pride instead in being a big fish in a small pond.

Billing $300K at 29 and managing 5 people is a good start (though you don't say what they bill). But it's only good, not great, and it's only a start. I know people years younger that are billing 3 times that. I mentor them currently . And they are furious with themselves for not being better. You are way too young to get this lazy mentally. Get out of your comfort zone...here are some goals.

- Bill $500K.
- Join the Pinnacle Society and get exposed to the people I'm talking about.
- Make placements at higher levels. C- and V-levels, Presidents. Change your power quotient.
- Double the per desk average (PDA) of your people in a year.

And lastly, give yourself a monetary goal that is not for you, but for others. Pick a charity or non-profit concern, or, better yet, start one, (I once started a theatre, later financed an independent movie) and then commit some money to them.

Some people go to the beach on vacation, look out at the ocean and are reminded of how insignificant they and their problems are. You need to hang with some big boys, and understand how much more you need to learn and see and do, before you have the luxury of burn out.

Not that I'm against burn out. If you burn out, it means, at least for a while, you were on fire.

Don't take the business or success for granted. It will soon humble you. You say you were once motivated by money but no so much now. That I get, especially if you have bought a lot of toys. But when I turned 30, I decided I had houses and cars and clothes, but not "screw you" money. Enough money to walk away from it all anytime I wanted. Once you have that, the world looks very different to you.

At 29, "screw you" money is a minimum of $3 million dollars. Get that done and then let's tackle boredom again.

Go for the Core

Dear Danny:

What do you think are the core competencies necessary in our business to compete now and in the future? I just finished reading, "The Core Competence of the Corporation", an article written by C. K. Prahalad and Gary Hamel in the Harvard Business Review and they believe that a core competence has to meet all three of the following:

1. Provides potential access to a wide variety of markets.

2. Should make a significant contribution to the perceived customer benefits of the end product.

3. Should be difficult for competitors to imitate.

This inspired my thinking about our industry's core competencies.

I'm interested in your perspective on this.

Thanks.

AccordingToDanny replies:

I would have to defer to the author Jim Collins, who wrote the seminal work, *Good to Great,* where he indeed tabbed "core competency" as one of the essential attributes of the most successful companies.

He called it the "hedgehog concept" (from the parable of the fox and the hedgehog: "The fox knows many things, the hedgehog knows only one thing, but knows it well. The hedgehog always wins.") To Collins, the keys are:

1) knowing what you are deeply passionate about.
2) knowing what you can be the best in the world at.
3) knowing what drives your economic engine.

Your core is where all three of these things intersect.

If you love recruiting life sciences people because you care deeply about what they do and when you're done working you go home and watch CSI, and you have a reputation (referenceable customers) and a database of strong candidates, and you are getting 30-33% fees which average over $25K...you have a hedgehog type core competency, and you'd be well advised to build on it. Hire more recruiters or researchers to increase your volume. Maybe stretch into academic research centers and not just hospitals, or go national rather than stay local, or work one or two levels above the functionality you are placing now, **but keep placing life sciences professionals, like the stoic, determined hedgehog you are.**

Hedgehogs don't get bored with their core competency. Recruiters do. That is their tragic flaw.

Reading for Rookies – Well... Not Just Rookies

Dear Danny:

Which books on basic sales skills do you recommend for a young rookie who is learning the business but has never sold before?

AccordingToDanny replies:

Now you're hitting me where I live. The only things in life I have found that can be loved unconditionally are dogs (in my case an Irish setter named Isaac), cats (2 Maine Coon Cats named Oscar and Zelda) and more to the point, words.

I look at it differently. Ziglar, Brian Tracey, Hopkins, even the early Robbins stuff is fine for basics. But to me that's like going to church and thinking you're doing your soul good because you've learned the songs, worn your best suit, or learned when to kneel.   Nothing matters beyond what's in your mind when you close your eyes.

Sales basics everyone knows in a week, and then spends a lifetime trying their damnedest not to practice them. Because they are afraid, because they have been taught not to bother anyone, because they are drawn to what is easy, and whatever else sales is, (empowering, enriching, electric), it is not easy.

So my rookies get the following reading list concurrently with my teaching of the basics. Do they follow up? Not many do. The ones that do read them have never regretted it.

Profiles in Courage by John F. Kennedy
Feel the Fear and Do it Anyway by Susan Jeffers
Resilience: The Power to Bounce Back When the Going Gets Tough! by Frederic Flach
Man's Search for Meaning by Vicktor Frankel

<u>Death of a Salesman</u> by Arthur Miller
<u>Theodore Rex</u> and <u>The Rise of Theodore Roosevelt</u> by
Edmund Morris
<u>Telling Lies</u> by Paul Eckman
<u>Days of Grace</u> by Arthur Ashe
<u>Seven Habits of Highly Effective People</u> by Steven Covey
<u>Rabbit is Rich</u> by John Updike

Once you're done with this list, you'll understand how your
clients and candidates feel, and you'll care about them, and
feeling and caring are the true basics of the excellent
salesperson. After you've done all this serious reading, take a
break and get anything by David Sedaris.

TELEPHONE

"Sometimes the sweetest sound on the planet... is a dial tone."

How Hard Can It be to Get Someone
 To Call Back?   p.145
The Thirty Second Commercial – Part One   p.147
The Thirty Second Commercial – Part Two   p.149
Help with Voice Mail   p.151
More on Voice Mail   p.154
How Vague on MPC Voice Mail?   p.156
It's Not the Fault of the MPC Call   p.159

143

How Hard Can It be to Get Someone to Call Back?

Dear Danny:

I am at a loss. I find that it is getting harder and harder to get anyone to call back, especially clients. I normally leave a full disclosure message with an MPC when marketing. Others have recommended leaving no messages but calling until you get the Hiring Manager on the phone, and others say to leave a nondescript sort of secretive message. What have you and your team found to be the best approach to getting Hiring Managers to return your calls or to get them live on the phone?

AccordingToDanny replies:

You know we advocate edgy MPC marketing, and our data supports that this is the most effective way. But the key is to be *edgy!* Most recruiters who send me calls have an overly serious, professional demeanor in their voice mail messages, and then loosen up when the client calls back.

You need to be just the opposite. Entertain on the message and then show them when they call back that along with being interesting and enthusiastic and fun to talk to, you're a pro as well.

"John, this is Danny Cahill, what did I ever do to you? You never write; you never call. Oh wait, I just remembered you don't know me. Here's the elevator pitch: I'm a recruiter that dominates your vertical, and I make these calls only when I think I can bring value to both of us. Last year the people I placed brought a combined $54 million dollars into the web analytic space, and I've recruited someone who's going to bring it to $60 million, and she could bring it to you. Reach out to me John, cold calling is sport, but it can be a contact sport."

That's a recent call nearly verbatim. Don't worry about the words, worry about the elements. Power, action oriented words delivered with some pop cultural or literary reference (let your wits exercise), backed with quantitative track record presented from their point of view. That's the formula.

Just to get you out of your funk, add one more element. Make your calls from 7:30-9:30AM and again 6-7:30 PM. The people you want are there then. Are you?

P.S. In follow up – please consider doing this. Leave two marketing voice mails at AccordingToDanny. One should be the one you are using now. The other should be a "new" style voice along the lines suggested above. I would love to have a chance to listen to and comment on them for you. To do this call us before 8:30 a.m. or after 5:00 p.m. ET at 203-439-0267 or call us during our regular business hours to arrange a specific time.

The Thirty Second Commercial – Part One

Dear Danny:

At the advice of my manager, I am attempting to write a 30 second commercial about myself. Il am doing this because my clients do not seem to be buying into the value of what I do and I have heard "what am I paying for?" from my clients. In the process, I have been looking for some industry standards to compare myself to. Where can I find some that don't involve shelling out a bunch of money?

Thanks, Danny!

AccordingToDanny replies:

A 30 second commercial is a great idea, even as an exercise so that you understand every day the "value prop" (as my software clients like to call it) that you take to the marketplace every day.

Standards of performance?

Most recruiters bill less than $150K. They are in business fewer than three years. There are only 75 members of the Pinnacle Society, the only association that verifies high production, and their standards include $1 million in revenue in three years. The CPC is the only professional designation you can get as a search professional. These are all standards you can measure yourself against and "brag about."

But try this instead. Call your contact or candidate on five of the deals you made, not recently, but in the last 2-3 years. Here's the key:

1) Get them to quantify the value in dollars that the company has received to date in terms of your candidate's contribution.

2) Ask for a written testimonial about the quality of your work as regards that investment.

I would rather your 30 second pitch say, *"rather than talk about myself, here's what others have received in the way of benefit from working with me and my firm."* If this is quantified, this kind of "performance-based" marketing can be powerful.

The best marketing is always your own good work...I'd be happy to review a draft.

The Thirty Second Commercial – Part Two

Dear Danny:

I'm taking you up on your offer. Here is my 30 second commercial:

30 Second Commercial for XYZ

I am a professional recruiter with a specialization in long-term administrative and manufacturing placements. My clients understand the value of the people who make up their organizations and cannot afford to make mistakes with this critical resource. My natural instincts about people allow me to find candidates that not only possess the background, skills, and experience required for the job but also the more intangible qualities like work ethic, personality, and attitude. Since I joined XYZ Resource Group in 2002, I have consistently met or exceeded performance standards set by Senior Recruiters with four or more years of experience. My reputation is continually growing as I provide consistent, reliable results for my clients.

AccordingToDanny replies:

Thanks for sending your call! Let's get to it. Why is it that some recruiters can read a well written pitch word for word 100 times a day and fail while some other recruiter can botch the numbers, reverse the syntax, slay the grammar, and get results?

Tone of voice, and the transference of energy via natural enthusiasm.

On a scale of 1-10, 10 being Al Sharpton on Ephedra, I would give you a solid 7.5. This means you could gear it up a notch, but you're close. Your voice as an instrument is excellent. There is a resonance, and unlike 99% of these we get sent to us, your pace and tempo was relaxed and unhurried. Very nice.

On to content. There are two things I would adjust:

a) It's a bit long. Until there is Voice Mail Ritalin, we need to hit it hard and fast. There are only two kinds of VM pitches, the quick and the dead.

b) While this will make my grad school profs cry out in pain, you need to forget some of the complete sentences and talk like you would to a friend. It comes across a tad stiff and "HRish." A Pinnacle member who has often billed$ 1 million a year says, *"You don't know me, but I have spent my life helping talented people look more forward to Mondays."* Your version is "my clients know the value of ..." You see? I love the middle part about ethics, not enough people add that, and talking about your natural abilities is a good idea too, but make it real. Like you're chatting.

c) (Okay, I lied, 3 things.) Don't say you've exceeded performance standards. Give me numbers. Do it in %'s. It will have more impact.

But I'm being picky. Overall, really good stuff. It needs a tweak, not an overhaul. You sound like you're on your game!

All the best.

Help with Voice Mail

Dear Danny:

I have been in the business for more than 15 years. Now, I find that I am leaving way too many voice mails. Not only that, I am not getting very many calls back. I have the same frustration whether it is a marketing or a recruiting call. Could you listen to my calls and give me some help?

(These are the transcripts of the calls.)

Recruiting:

Good morning Danny. My name is Beth. Would you please call me? My telephone number is 123-456-7890.

The reason that I'm calling – I'm working on a project. It's time sensitive, and I'd like to talk to you as soon as possible. Thank you.

Again, it's Beth. 123-456-7890.

Marketing:

Good morning Danny. My name is Beth. I'm with XYZ Group. Would you please call me? I have a candidate who comes from your industry and I think you'd like to hear about her.

Please call at 123-456-7890.

It's Beth. Thank you.

AccordingToDanny replies:

You might have gotten away with this type of Voice Mail approach five years ago...but no longer. Voice mail has exploded. **Hardly anybody can refrain from hitting the delete key if they feel they are being sold something…anything!!**

The other sweeping change is that if I can't tell what your call is about, then I also hit the delete key. **Curiosity and professional courtesy are poor motivators for call backs in the new age of voice mail.**

I tell you this because in your voice mails:

- It's not clear at all what you do or what you're about.
- You just use your first name which is a tip off to a "sell."
- You use passive language. "Would you call me back?"
- You're uncertain, "I think."
- There is no description of the "sizzle" or compelling story of your candidate.
- You say, "The reason I'm calling." This is also a tip off to being sold. This is also a redundant phrase that you should lose. You're just stalling and steeling your never when using it. Whatever you say after you say, "The reason I'm calling…" *is* the reason you're calling

I think your voice quality is excellent. It's resonant and clear. And I like that you give your number upfront.

But you need to add:

- A short credibility statement about you and your firm.
- A short compelling story of a candidate, if marketing, or a client's attributes, if recruiting.

152

In this day and age, people respond to targeted, specific situations. A hot candidate, a job about to be filled. You need to create energy and urgency and this transference of passion will get calls back.

In the surveys I've done with our clients, the number one reason for calling back on a marketing call was the candidate's track record.

The number two reason? Like the sirens in Ulysses, the personality of the recruiter was too engaging not to respond to.

That's where you need to go...

More on Voice Mail

Dear Danny:

When leaving a voice mail to attract candidates, how much detail do you leave in the message? My co-workers and I go back and forth on what method gets the best callback percentages?

AccordingToDanny replies:

In a world where the estimate is that 83% of all calls made in a business day end up in voice mail, this is a key skill to master. Keep in mind that "what" you say is not even in the same league with "how" you say it.

You must:

- be wildly enthusiastic without being Jim Carey cartoonish.
- be confident and serene about who you are and the value inherent in talking to you.
- assume they are having a grey, grim day and you will change that right NOW.

That said, we favor the direct approach. Give them a taste of why your search is a singularly spectacular opportunity, but don't give so much that there's no reason to call you back. Some recruiters leave so much detail that the candidate can figure out where it is, goes to the company Website, and posts their resume without even calling you back. With that, you become a non-profit organization.

So here's a recent recruiting voice mail from my office:

"Jeff, you and I haven't spoken before, but you may have heard of me or my firm. This is Bill XYZ from Hobson Associates. We're one of the oldest and largest privately-held search firms in America that specializes in sales talent. I work only in supply chain and only in your sector, the retail space. I'm going to fill a VP of Sales search for one your direct competitors in the near future, a company that has grown 15% in each of the last two years when others have been floundering, a company written up in Forbes and Money because they have proprietary software that rocks and a management team that has a track record for making millionaires. I have no idea how your current or future situation stacks up, but consider this call opportunity knocking. I'm in until Noon today, 123-456-7890..."

Remember: energy, passion, confidence.

How Vague on MPC Voice Mail?

Dear Danny:

I know that you and some of the other trainers out there endorse leaving a vague voice mail message with hiring managers and candidates, instead of the more traditional MPC-type message.

We have been trying this with mixed results. There is no doubt that we get more return calls with our vague message. However, it is not unusual for a VP of Sales to call back and once he realizes that he may have been tricked, snookered, mislead, or whatever you want to call it, into calling back, to lose his cookies on the recruiter or receptionist.

I realize that the whole world is leaving an MPC message and that the Hiring Managers delete most of them as soon as they realize what the call is about. However, we have found it a better (smoother/cleaner, etc.) way to initiate a working relationship. Even though it is the equivalent of spilling your popcorn in the lobby before the movie even starts.

So, here is my question. What exactly do you say (or could you say) in a voice mail message to get the call back volume that we would like from the vague version and still get off to a good start with the Hiring Manager without the risk of them feeling deceived or us apologizing for or explaining the vague voice mail?

AccordingToDanny replies:

Although I personally have always been more effective leaving a message that requires a call back to satisfy the curiosity I try to build up without being flippant or "cutesy" (and I want to add here that "rusing", the time dishonored practice of pretending to be someone you're not to get past a gatekeeper or get a call back, will get you fired in my office in a NY minute), we track the numbers of returned voice mails calls in my office and there is no doubt that in our survey of the methods we use to get clients to call back on voice mail, the undisputed champ was: the abbreviated MPC call.

Not your whole pitch. If you leave your whole pitch, the only reason to call back is if they have an exact opening for that exact candidate, and while its true that in a country of 280 million people a one in a million chance happens 280 times a day, I wouldn't want to pay my bills by playing these kinds of odds.

Truncate it. Accent the achievements. Quantify. Translate these numbers in a way that is beneficial to your client.

"Jeff, let's bottom line this. You don't know me and you won't return this call without a good reason. I recently recruited a candidate for a competitor of yours who is kicking butt in the Mid-Atlantic territory to the tune of$ 6 million dollars since January. He has busted his quota 11 consecutive quarters and under the right circumstances, he could be doing it for you. I'm here until 3 today, 432-890-2121...."

You say your VPs of Sales get mad when they feel they've been deceived or played with. That's because they are like you: mavericks, numbers oriented, money motivated, and they love to be sold. We find that if you let a client, especially in sales, know you are trying to sell him and will do so in an enthusiastic, fun way, they are responsive.

But along with your style, your energy and your sense of humor, you have to have the goods - a quality, recruited candidate that can make or save them money.

I think a vague, or even provocative message was more effective just a couple of years ago when there was less inundation of voice mail. Now, unless you are a BIG personality and are ON all the time, you need an MPC, a person with a life situation and an agenda, and a time frame. Hiring authorities are problem solving opportunists. It's in their nature to respond.

It's Not the Fault of the MPC (Most Placeable Candidate) Call

Dear Danny:

I make MPC calls. I don't get calls back. Now, let me tell you about a recent incident that makes me wonder whether or not the MPC call is the way to go.

About my niche, it is high tech sales. My calls are made to VPs of Sales - no HR people on my list. My calls are MPC calls only. In addition to what I have written, I took the liberty of sending you an example of the call I make so you can hear what I am saying.

This is the incident. Earlier this week, I went to a business meeting where I was able to meet, face-to-face, many of the VPs of Sales that I have been calling. When I introduced myself, each of them told me that they knew my name and remembered my having called them, even telling me how many voice mails I had left for them. I asked them why they didn't call back. All but one told me they hit delete as soon as they find out that the call is from a recruiter. They all observed they get too many of these calls to even bother to listen to them through - too busy selling to hear out a recruiter voice mail. One even told me he had hired a former recruiter to handle the hiring in his company. Rather than deleting the message, he sends it to this HR guy who never calls back.

So it seems like the MPC call is not getting their attention. Is there another way, another call type to make?

I heard about a successful salesperson who sometimes sends a pair of new shoes to his prospect hiring managers (all at very high levels) and then follows up with a call. When he calls they tend to take the call because they are curious about the guy who sent them the shoes.

I track my numbers and the last 400 MPC calls have yielded 2 job orders. If I were working for you and walked into your office to tell you this information and sent you this call, what would you advise?

AccordingToDanny replies:

400 calls and 2 job orders? If you did that here, I would tell you to take a day off or have a drink. Or both! This business just isn't that hard!!!

I want to attack this in two ways. We'll talk about modifying your voice mail approach, because it can be easily refined, but let's discuss some market realities first.

- Voice mail is extremely prevalent and getting worse, so no solution will be perfect.
- You are calling Sales VPs who are on the road and selling, so for you the problem is worse.
- You need to vary how you go about getting jobs.

Our research shows that there are many ways recruiters are getting jobs:

- Marketing Calls
- From interviewing candidates
- Web Postings
- Trade Shows
- Split Groups
- Outbound marketing – a nice way to say spam
- Hire a PR firm to position to the firm.

You must strategically divide up your business development time among the various methods. A typical recruiter here will make 25 marketing calls a day with MPCs, then follow up a trade show list, check ten Web Postings, and use

Internet or active candidates to find where the jobs aremarketing calls with MPCs, then follow up a trade show list, check 10 Web postings, and use Internet or active candidates as a way to find out where the jobs are. Of course, we will call no companies the active candidates are currently vying for, but if their candidacy is decided or they have no interest, we will pursue those jobs. One of my clients reports a full third of his firm's jobs come from turning a reference check into a marketing call. is percentage of return calls on reference checks? 90%! I like those odds.

Now, the call you sent me. Your VPs say they hang up or hit delete as soon as they hear it's a recruiter. If that is true, then it's not the MPC part of the call that is not effective. They're NOT hearing that part of the call; they're gone by then! (Incidentally, we had a VP of Sales in our Rookie Retreat of last week, and he said the ONLY calls he responds to are MPC calls.)

The problem is you have 10-15 seconds MAX to engage. Then they decide to keep listening or to go away.

I'm going to suggest something and you are going to be uncomfortable with it. THAT'S GOOD. You're comfortable with your approach, and it's not working. So let's try something different. I want you to exaggerate this for a couple of weeks and your natural personality will bring you back to the middle.

Your calls are way, way too long. You don't get to the sizzle of the candidate until it's too late, and you speak in proper, well composed, complete sentences. You tell the VP you "were compelled" to present this individual.

You and I have spoken in person at seminars and on the phone in Webex meetings. In fact, you complimented me on my associates, Amy and Bob, when we last met. You walked up to me and said, (paraphrasing), "Gotta tell you, Amy is super, and Bob, he does right by you." You didn't say, "Mr. Cahill, I feel compelled to comment on your staff."

You need to get conversational.

You need to be outrageous in the first 10 seconds. (During the recent war, one of my recruiters was promoting an MPC who would lead a "shock and awe" campaign against their competitors.) Say, "Mr. ____ you should NOT call most headhunters back. I'm not most headhunters." Try our new one, "Mr. ____, every night before I go to sleep I can talk to God, but I can't get YOU on the phone, you want to explain that?"

You need to use more POWER words - a little hyperbole and shameless promotion about your MPC can go a long way. You need to be BIG, BOLD, and DIFFERENT - remember, exaggerate this. I want you to feel foolish at first. You'll feel better when you get your first call back.

We had a contest recently for the most original voice mail, $100 to the winner. Just to show you we practice what we preach, here is the winning entry:

"____, my candidate has been a consistent CASH COW for your direct competitor. In fact, wait, I can hear him coming now. Listen?..MOOOOOOOOO!!!

We fight this battle every day with you. I suggest you vary your biz dev attack by balancing the other methods we outlined, and make your voice mails shorter, crisper, and use language that you are not comfortable with. Try some hipster slang. Aging baby boomer clients love it.

But remember, don't blame your MPC. Very few of the 400 people you have called heard anything about your MPC.

COLLECTED ESSAYS

"Writing is the only thing I do, that when I'm doing it, I don't feel I should be doing something else."

Ernest Hemingway

Collected Essays

These essays were originally published in the quarterly newsletter of The Pinnacle Society and are reprinted with its permission.

Did I Say that Out Loud?	p. 167
You're Just Like Me Only Different	p .177
Pivotal People	p. 181
Retaining Top Recruiters	p. 185
Gospel of Gossip	p .189
Brother's Keeper	p .193

165

Did I Say That Out Loud?

What was I thinking while I dialed the phone, and began the most humiliating day of my work life? *Was* I thinking? After ten years as a headhunter, pounding out calls between 8:30 a.m. and Noon, what we call, "Prime Calling hours", is it possible I didn't have a thought in my head? I suspect it's just the opposite. Tons of thoughts, none of them connected, all running through my head as I sleepwalked my way through the part of my day that makes me money and keeps me alive. The night before we had argued mildly. Halfway through the video we had rented, an incoherent affair, she said, "he hasn't made a decent movie since Gilbert Grape." Which would have been fine had we been watching a Johnny Depp movie, but she said this during a close up of Keanu Reeves. I corrected her. She said it was petty for me to do so and beside the point. "Not," I assured her, "to Johnny Depp, it's not."

The phone was now ringing. Like a man stuck in traffic, late for a meeting, flapping his legs back and forth and pounding the steering wheel, who doesn't know he is forty-five seconds away from a tractor trailer jack knifing in front of him, I had no idea how close I was to career ruin.

I could blame technology. I have developed a nasty habit of reading my emails while I make my calls. Despite the filtering software we have added, I still am asked daily if I want to enlarge my penis "without those nasty hanging weights,", and with no "time consuming pumping machines." The proper, morally contained use of hyperbole and manipulation are tools of any headhunter's trade, and the skilled salesperson in me had to smile when I read the shrewd copy, " we know you've read that size doesn't matter to women, and we know that you know that she knows you need to hear that lie." Or I could blame the advent of voice mail. When I started, you called someone and they picked up the phone. You had them. Or you got their secretary, which was fine, because I quickly developed the thrust and parry, the gamesmanship, and the nuances of flirting, so common among unattractive men. And they put me through or got me a call back from their bosses.

Now no one picks up his or her phone. Nearly *every* call ends up in voice mail. I knew Jonathan Hennessy wouldn't be any different. I had called him three times that week. It should have been safe for my mind to wander; it should have been okay for me to lose focus for a moment. I shouldn't have to sit here and try to remember what my thoughts were at that moment. After a decade of working here, I have earned the right not to be defensive.

"Hi, you've reached Jonathan Hennessy, Director of Global Marketing, and I am either on the phone or away from my desk. Please leave a message, and I'll get back to you as soon as I can. Thanks for calling."

Do you understand that I can spend all day making phone calls and never speak to a soul, and that can be, depending on mood and circumstance, crushingly depressing, or hugely exhilarating? That there are days where you feel you could and should be replaced by a machine that dials these numbers and leaves your script and just as many days when this absence of intimacy makes you feel invincible? You can do your job, even be successful, and give none of your true self. Some days that seems like such a gift.

Be that as it may. Enter Career Meltdown.

"Jonathan, good morning, it's Jesse Kinsella, Management Source Consulting . I wanted to get back to you on Terry Matthews. I met with him yesterday, checked his references, and I think we should go forward to the interview stage. So call me when you get this, 203-234-5476, and we'll set something up. I'm here all day. Thanks Jonathan, take care. Love you."

And I hung up.

I said, *love you,* and then hung up.

To Jonathan Hennessy. A Client at a key account. Someone I have talked to exactly twice for a total of four minutes, and *that* was on a conference call with three other recruiters.

Take care, love you.

Calm down, I told myself, as my chest tightened and the back of my head started to tingle. You know how you are. You imagine things all day long. You daydream. It's conceivable that in one of these dreams you would wonder to yourself how easy it would be to freak out a male client you hardly know by casually leaving *love you* on their voice mail, but you would never say it. No one would actually say it. So take a moment. Breathe. Pretend you're in the last 5 minutes of the Yoga class you take at the gym, and you're doing mountain pose, the one configuration you can do without resembling a mannequin, and ask yourself the key goddamn question:

Did I say that out loud?

"Juxtaposition, Kinsella. Meditate at home, phone calls at work. Juxtaposition."

That would be my boss, displaying his two talents. He has a large vocabulary he never gets to exercise running a search firm, and he hates to see recruiters off the phone. After ten years and the small fortune I've made him, I still feel guilty all day when he catches me dogging it. I'm tempted to ask him for help. I would never feed his ego by admitting this in front of him, but I have seen him get us out of some pretty hairy situations with clients, often with solutions that were so clever there's no way you would have thought of them yourself. But first I would have to endure some analysis. The boss is a Self Help junkie, and would run me through 5 steps to facing fear, or a step-by-step guide to peak performance

169

through breathing before he would tell me what to do. I can handle this myself.

I pull up the company on my screen, and check the contact file. Sometimes we list the secretary's name in the comments section. Yes! I get her on the first ring. She is friendly and sounds like she's having a good day. I'm going to pull this off. I explain I was talking to Jonathon and got cut off, and that I'm about to get on a plane, might I have his cell? No problem.

If I get him live, I'm going to put on a show. I had my wife on the other line. No, even better. I had the florist on the other line, who is sending flowers to my wife, because we had a fight, (a little truth thrown in often cushions a lie), and they were asking me what to put on the card just as your voice mail beeped, and I juxtaposed (thanks boss) the two conversations, so now my wife is getting flowers that say, "Pleasure doing business with you."

I get his cell voice mail. This throws me off. I have to give this context.

"Jonathan, Jesse Kinsella again. Or maybe not again, depending on if you checked your voice mail. I just left you a message and I need to explain it, because I'm sitting here mortified and embarrassed..."

Whoa, what was that crackle? Oh no, don't lose the signal on me. Give me fifteen seconds, I can get this done.

"Look, let me bottom line this, because I can tell the signal is weak, I left you a message saying I loved you, which obviously I shouldn't have done. I don't mean shouldn't have done because it wasn't the right time or forum to express some inner, true feelings, I mean, 'didn't mean it', meaning I was distracted and that's not to say, since I am totally unaware of your...history or predilections...okay this phone is totally dead, and for all I know all you heard is me

170

repeating that I loved you and now I've become a telestalker."

Well, now it doesn't matter if I said it out loud before. Because that time I definitely said it out loud. Time to cut my losses, endure some Chopra, and see the boss...

"Interesting. This is definitely an alpha level of consciousness. That's the right brain, where all the creativity is. I just went to a Mind Control seminar on how to solve problems like this by tapping at will into the right brain."

"Great. So what does your right brain say?"

"You're screwed."

"Oh I see, you need to enjoy this first."

"Technically, we have some legal exposure. This is sexual harassment. You have created a hostile working environment for him. Poor guy can't check his voice mail or his cell without you hitting on him."

"Could we hurry this along? Hennessy could pick up his messages at any time and then I don't need to be in here getting abuse."

"Okay. Here's the real deal. You created this to avoid working. Your mind didn't slip. This wasn't a mistake. It was a way, a creative way, I will grant you, to sabotage your own success. You didn't want to work today, so you created this crisis."

I got up, started out, and then walked in three little circles around my chair.

"That is such crap. I cannot tell you how angry you've just made me."

"That's because it's true. You're not angry at me; you're angry at the truth."

"No, I'm pretty sure it's you. Why don't you take a break from the mind control seminars and make a hundred calls a day? See if you can keep everything straight. Okay, that's *not* how I meant that. Thanks for all your help."

"Jesse. Relax, this will blow over. If you want me to call him, I will. We'll have a few laughs at your expense and this will become a war story."

"You know him?"

"I've met him. He's very cute. But listen, I'm not kidding. I don't believe words slip out. Not a single one. I believe they fight their way out. The important ones get past the gatekeeper."

"Was that written on the calendar that came with your registration package?"

I went back to my desk and checked my messages. Nothing from Hennessy. I could try writing an email. No loss of signal, complete control of the message, and best of all, no having to deal with his responses in real time. But what if he's a High Touch/Low Tech guy who only communicates via phone or cell, and relies on his secretary to respond to his email? What if she's a gossip? Or worse, what if they're having an affair and she thinks I'm a threat?

Selma popped up from the cubicle in front of me, disconnected the wire from her headset to her phone, and headed off toward the kitchen. That meant it was 11:30, and her second cup of black coffee. She is extremely disciplined, and no doubt why she's one of the top producers and youngest junior partners. She leaves the headset on her head as proof she's still in attack mode, and won't take it off until she leaves early this evening. She's very businesslike on the phone, and yet isn't above flirting with the VPs and Presidents she sells to, accenting her reinforcement of their charm and youthful vigor with a phony laugh that makes the rest of us roll our eyes. Selma is no fool. She's a team player as well. She'll have an answer for me.

Selma set her 16 oz. cup of Green Mountain French Vanilla coffee down, and leaned back in the conference room chair I had ushered her into. She folded her hands.

"You have to blow him."

"Beg pardon?"

"You heard me. Jess, it's a rolling retainer for 10 Director level jobs, it's worth $300K in fees. That's like $100K for every minute you're on your knees. This is a no brainer."

"You realize, putting business ethics aside for a moment, that I'm married, as well as a raging heterosexual?"

"I don't see any of those things as deal breakers. Look, I have a Webcast in like ten minutes."

Selma bounded out of the conference room, and I couldn't help but feel an odd respect for her. She evaluates, decides, pulls the trigger, and doesn't look back. All I do is look back, and not only do I not like what I see, but I have no idea what's passing me by in the meantime.

There was a knock on the conference room door. Jennifer leaned in, and said, "Jonathan Hennessy is on for you. I told him you were in a conference, but he said he'd like to wait."

In Little League, when I was 10, I peed my pants in the dugout. This is shameful in and of itself, but I knew my shame would be limited, since I never left the bench, given my inability to catch, hit, run or throw. An inning later, Coach Baker told me to pinch hit for Paul Cifaldi. I strode to

173

the plate, my pants soaked, and I can still hear the laughter, the parents' pity, and the catcher's soulful, "EWWW." When I walked back to the dugout, three swings later, Coach Baker said, "You gotta learn to hold it, or tell the truth, but this stuff in the middle ain't gonna work." Thirty years later, it was time to learn that lesson.

"Mr. Hennessy, it's Jesse, I wanted to..."

"...Terry Matthews, right? I saw the resume. He does look good. Can he get in here next Wednesday, say around 2 p.m.?"

"I'm sure he can. I'll set it up."

Is this possible? Is he going to bury it? Is he sending me a message by keeping this all business? Is he saying, "Look, I understand, let's not even go there?" Could he be that generous a spirit?

"So, Jesse, let's talk about the message you left me earlier."

Please let me die. I just want to die.

"I couldn't call you right back because I needed to think a little bit. It made me feel very odd. A few years ago I went through what's commonly called a nasty divorce. I meant to get back in the game right away but with IPOs and flying to vendors in Japan and scramble tournaments...it just never happened. Partly that's because I never changed any of the things that drove my wife nuts, and they were the same things that drove my first wife nuts. The kids took their mom's side, and they were right to, but now they won't talk to me. You don't wake up one day and characterize yourself as lonely. You get a call from a headhunter, who is clearly distracted and confusing his last call with his next call, and you hear words you haven't heard in a very long time. And you play the voice mail twice, so you can hear the words again, even though you're not their intended recipient. And you feel better, nonetheless. You still there, Jesse?"

"Yes sir."

"Lost all respect for me now, have you?"

"No sir, gaining it, exponentially, in fact."

"Still love me, do you?"

"No sir, I'm over you now."

"Get Matthews in here on Wednesday."

Your're Just Like Me.. Only Different

At AccordingToDanny, my training company, we track just about everything. I'm both oral aggressive and anal retentive, making it possible for my psychotherapist to have several homes mortgage free, and impossible for my employees, who after all do the actual hard work of tracking and collecting data, to get a good night's sleep.

When I compare the "Ask Danny's" and the "requests for mentoring" that I get from the population of recruiters at large, and then compare that to the requests I get from top producers, including the members of our society, there is more that unites us than divides us (sorry, too much NPR during a presidential election year)

What unites us?

All recruiters ask:

About absurd and ridiculous placement situations, brought on sometimes by our own error or a lapse in judgment or salesmanship, and sometimes, well...stuff happens. It's the nature of our business, and is part of what makes it glorious. Today's labyrinth like miasma is tomorrow's badge of excellence and treasured, if embellished, memory.

About contracts, legal exposure, non-competes, employment agreements, and the interpretation of offer letters and their various covenants. Our CPC designation is often scoffed at, usually by those without the letters after their name, but the things I learned there I use every day. These questions serve as a reminder as well that we are not lawyers, are vulnerable to changes in law and the back door approaches of lobbyists. If you read these questions as much as I do, you'd join NAPS or your local state association fast, as they all have an ethics chair, and a government regulations chair, which is code for lobbyist negotiator.

177

About fees. The most arrogant of top billers and the most lowly of neophytes get on the phone with their clients and with alarming regularity, fold like cheap suits. At least the rookies admit they got overwhelmed or lacked the skill, the top producers are lazy and acting expediently. Their principles seldom survive a looming bad month.

About how to leave better voice mails. We are talking to less and less people every day. We yell out into the night, "it's a phone business, its about touching people." And it is. But with the exception of the recently retired Concorde, no improved technology has ever been put back in the bottle. We won't stop hitting titanium rackets on the tennis court no matter how much it corrupts the game, we aren't going to stop driving our cars because highways get crowded, and people are not going to stop using their voice mail systems. It is in fact no longer **just** a phone business! That is perfectly obvious and yet we are coming in tomorrow and hitting our desks and preparing for phone time, because we know no other way. **We are living in the in-between time, the changing of the guard in how people communicate, and to be more precise, how people sell during the work day.** What % will be Email? Instant messaging? Trade Shows? Webcasts? It's not known yet, and we need to make a living now. So we pound the phone. And it works, at least in a good market. But underneath we can all feel something is slipping, something doesn't make sense. I think all we can do is stay open to change, and when the new paradigm becomes clear, have the guts to go with it.

About getting retainers. I am currently personally mentoring two Pinnacle members in this area. It scares them. They want verbiage and collateral material and surefire, paint by number approaches. I share my PowerPoint, and they act like I have given them gold.

But every retainer I get, and I'm pitching one Wednesday in NYC, I get because:

178

1) I believe I should get paid for my work.
2) They are buying my commitment, and as any one of my ex-girlfriends or wives can tell you, that's not easy to get. (When "client-money" is invented by some Marvin Mitchelson sycophant, I really will have to hang it up.)
3) I don't give any other option. It's not "retainer or contingency", it's "this is how I work." The one way, the true way.
4) I am so niched I can do it faster than anyone else.
5) I will present a short list of candidates.
6) I will hold you and you will hold me to a prescribed timeline.
7) The best candidates will not talk to me if I am not retained. Your retainer dollars buys you access to the best.

If you aren't getting retainers you are violating or hedging one or more of the above precepts.

What divides us?

Ironically, the members of the society, and many other top producers I know who, for any number of reasons, don't seek membership, are more jaded about their careers. They have changed lives, made or are making a fortune, have a place of status and power in the world, and do so every day in air conditioned offices that they drive to in executive suites on wheels, and yet are the ones that ask me the most about balance, about slumps, about the crushing tediousness of the business, the lying candidates and the harsh, discarding nature of capitalism.

The rookies and the underachievers? They would kill to have the skills and gifts we take for granted. They don't ask "is this all there is?" They think, "this is wonderful, I just wish I were better."

179

There is a Japanese fish that, if you put in a 6-inch bowl, will grow to 4 inches. If you put it in an 18- inch bowl, it will grown to 12 inches, and if you put it in a 4- foot wide tank, it will grow to 3 feet.

Most recruiters have no choice. They try as hard as they can and grow to the size of their bowl. Pinnacle people have a choice. They need to get out of the bowl and find the widest tank possible. They are that blessed. And cursed.

Pivotal People

So I'm at this conference, prepared to do what my recruiters affectionately call my dogma and pony show. My session is at 10:15. I'm the breakout guy at this conference because it's not in the staffing industry. If you're Steve McQueen, breakout guy means you have the lead and your name on the marquee. If you're the breakout guy at a conference, it means "keep improving and we might give you a keynote, but in the meantime, thank your lucky stars you're not 'Roundtable Guy.' " Roundtable Guy is a notch above Luncheon Speaker, but it's a close call.

Anyway, I get up early to ride the lifecycle, do yoga, and eat oatmeal. And then I remember how much I hate all three of those choices, and decided to go downstairs instead, ostensibly to see the keynote speaker, but also hoping that they're serving something greasy for breakfast, which I can eat and rationalize because I'm "on the road." This is my first rationalization of the day and it's not yet 8:30. What's wrong with me? I'm usually in double figures by now.

I walk into Ballroom A (my own session is in the "Windtree Room" – Breakout Guys don't get letters after the name of their room), and within ten seconds I catch the vibe. Everyone wants to see this speaker. People are "pumped" about this guy. I check the brochure on the seat next to me. Never heard of him. Some doctor. I read the bio and then the word jumps out at me and I understand what the fuss is about.

He's been on Oprah. A lot. Dr. Phil. Everyone in the place knows this but me, and I suddenly feel the way I do when there is a crowd on the first tee on a Tuesday afternoon, "Doesn't anybody work for a living?"

How are all these people watching Oprah? Doesn't matter. The introduction is finished and the roar is not for Dr. Phil, it

181

is really for Oprah. George Bush may have his finger on the button, but Oprah runs the country.

And this guy got me. It's why I speak, and why we all go to speakers. Sometimes they get you. Right where you live. The good ones are soothsayers, magicians; you think they have been following you around. They "bore" through you like a laser beam.

He said we all have three "Pivotal People" in our lives. Three people of such immense influence that we return to them in our minds whenever we're at a crossroad. A coach, a priest, a parent. He asked us to shut our eyes and think about our three pivotal people. (I kept my eyes open and watched, and sure enough, he left the stage. Probably had a cheeseburger. It's an old trick. Audience participation exercises are the TV timeouts of speaking.)

At first, I was depressed. I didn't have three pivotal people. No one that I could remember would rise to his definition of "major influences".

I had the movies. I've always lived largely in my imagination, and I don't know if it's tragic or not that my influences are fictional, and I'll probably never know. (My therapist will kill me if I bring it up; her "to do" list for me makes the Koran look like a cake recipe.)

I'm not alone. Salman Rushdie claims that "The Wizard of Oz" made a writer out of him. The movie "Bambi" wreaked havoc on the deer hunting industry. Jennifer Beal's outfits in "Flashdance" sent posh boutiques scrambling for raggedy workout clothes. Sales of Mozart's recordings were in a 200 year slump when "Amadeus" came out in 1984 and turned everything around for the old boy.

So my Pivotal People, whom I have turned to in the recent turbulent market, are from the movies. I have many more than three, but for the current times, consider the following:

Pivotal Person #1 for a bad market... Harrison Ford. The scene in the "The Fugitive". Tommy Lee Jones has a gun on him. Ford can surrender, or he can leap down a waterfall that makes Niagara Falls look like a shower head. He tells Tommy Lee he didn't kill his wife. And it is Tommy Lee's answer that has kept me in good stead when everyone tells me, in their negative, cynical way: 1) there are no job orders, 2) they won't pay fees, 3) there is no business. It is Tommy Lee I turn to when my people tell me they are tired, they are scared, they are broken. It is Tommy Lee I recall when my senior person tells me that he can get a retainer if I would just allow a refund guarantee. Tommy Lee who comes to mind when this same recruiter intimates that maybe they are burned out and can't go on UNLESS I cut this deal... Tommy Lee said... I DON'T CARE!

Pivotal Person #2... Woody Allen, the man who says his one regret in life is that he is not someone else, a man thrown out of college because he cheated on his metaphysics test by looking within the soul of the boy next to him... when I feel sorry for myself that the world is harder now than it used to be, that there has to be an easier way... I think of Woody in "Annie Hall", when he explained the nature of gratitude. "There are basically two kinds of people. The terrible and the miserable. The terrible are like crippled or blind people, I don't know how they do it, and the miserable... are EVERYONE ELSE... so you should be happy that you're miserable." And so I am...

Pivotal Person #3... Bill Murray in "Tootsie"... because it reminds me what I really love about the business. The goofiness of it. I am paid to live by my wits. That's incredible to me even after 19 years. Every day it's a game on the phone. My first phone call, in 1982, the very first one I ever made, upon answering, the receptionist said, "May I help you?" And I replied, "Ma'am, you have to trust me, there is no help for me." And she laughed. And she put me through. Bill Murray plays a playwright in "Tootsie," and in my pivotal scene he is explaining to a girl at a party, "I don't want them to walk out saying it's a good play. I don't care if they walk out saying it's a bad play. I want them walking out saying, "What was that?"' And that's been my goal ever since.

At an intersection in Hollywood there is graffiti, on a sign, that says, "Everything you need to learn you can get from the films of John Hughes." Well, I wouldn't go that far. But comfort comes in all forms. My influences are not flesh and blood and I don't call them. I insert them and rewind and play them.

Perhaps now, as the market stubbornly, sluggishly stalls, it makes sense to recall an unlikely Pivotal Person. Big Arnold... sunglasses and black leather jacket, leaning over the cop in "Terminator" and promising... "I'll be Back."

As will we all...

Retaining Top Recruiters

Many Pinnacle members run their desks, as well as manage
a team of recruiters. Most would agree that the former is a
far easier task than the later. At its worst, managing
recruiters feels like nothing more than the baby-sitting of
spoiled brats, the constant propping up of fragile egos. This,
of course, seemed a fair and just system when we were the
brats with the egos, but once we reach the ranks of
management, the system seems badly flawed. Many believe
that marginal recruiters make the best managers, and that
top producers are too self-involved to manage, and have
too little patience to teach. Since we can make oodles of
money just making placements, why would we bother?

Last week, I took some of my senior recruiters to the NAPS
convention in New Orleans, where I was doing the keynote
speech. We went out to Bourbon Street to release some
demons, and I, of course, being of an advanced age and
possessing an amateur liver, went home early (2:00 a.m., but
this the Big Easy).

The next day, after my speech, a gentleman came up to me
and said he had "picked the brains of my recruiters" to see
what my firm was really like. "Christ," he said, "They would
take a bullet for you."

As I would for them. I have a core of 10 people who have
been around a very long time.

We have a junior class that 3-7 years' experience. It's a cliché
to say we are a family, though we are, and a very
dysfunctional one. More to the point, we are a culture.
There is a Hobson point of view, a Hobson "auteur theory"
that is hard to explain. Suffice it to say that most people
believe happiness lies in the giving and getting of love, and
while we at Hobson value those things, the people I have
made successful prefer Aristotle's definition of happiness: "The

exercise of vital powers, along lines of excellence, in a life affording them scope."

Here are some of the keys to my success in retaining key people, three of whom have been here since Ronald Reagan's first term.

A career track. You start here as a recruiter, you become an associate with certain privileges, then a senior associate, and then can be nominated for partnership, and then senior partnership. These last two are full equity positions. If you quit, or I fire you, you still own your piece of my firm. We grant partnerships sparingly, and people are driven to achieve them. Should I sell, you hit a home run. We are in it together. The rest of the industry is nothing more than a feudal system from the Middle Ages. His Lordship and his workers. Doesn't work.

I ask people how they like to be managed, and then I manage them in just the opposite manner. (Example: "I like being left alone. I'm not the kind who responds to day-to-day fussing." I'm all over this character like sweat. Recruiters try to push away what they know is good for them.)

Child Voice/Adult Voice... if a recruiter gives me emotional feedback, I go "strictly bix" on them, and if I'm getting a non-emotional, analytical reasoning for their issue, I go emotional. Parents do this well and it breaks through the wall of indifference.

There are four forms of "Kick Ass."

    a)   You need to do X production and you need to do it by X (imply "or else").
    b)   You disappoint me. I love you. You hurt me. Please produce and end the pain.
    c)   Karma... you have gifts. You are squandering them. You will pay a heavy price.

d)   Lost Sale... this is my fault, how did I screw you up?
I'm a bad manager.

Use these sparingly. There are subtle shades of each. With
experience, you mix and match. A lost Sale/Karma can
sound like a Sharpton rally if done well!

Criticize in Private; Praise in Public... Use a 3:1 ratio – for
every negatively charged private meeting you have, you
should praise them publicly three times.

(*** An exception would be a Prima Donna. Criticize him or
her publicly so everyone knows no one is above the law. ***)

When things are Bad... Get Silly. Show some faith, spend
some money, close the office, take everyone out for a drink.
"In a hundred years, we'll all be dead" can reignite a staff
afraid to incur your wrath.

When things are Good... Get Mad. Push. My people say, I'm
never satisfied, nothing is ever good enough. They're right,
and the day they feel there's nothing to push for, they don't
need me, and I have no relevance.

It's okay not to know the answers, but it's not okay to not
know who you are. Be consistent and your flaws will be
endearing. If you are erratic and unpredictable in a biz that
is uncertain, you're not meant to lead.

In the end there are two kinds of leaders. The kind that feel
the heat and the kind that see the light. I made a list the
other night of the 25 funniest moments of my life. I'm not
that easy to make laugh, and so the times when I have
doubled over, stopped breathing, and begged someone to
shut up or I might laugh to death are few. And precious.
Seventeen of them happened during the work day with my
staff. Five of them happened this year. Who knows about
next year? I'm smiling thinking about it...

Gospel of Gossip

A recruiter of mine looked me in the eye and said, with big doleful eyes, "can you keep a secret?" And I said, "of course" and he proceeded to disappoint me with news I had already gleaned from a combined strategy of eavesdropping, minor bribery, and hanging around the company cafeteria ,which you must do in my company to avoid being talked about. And even then, you must keep moving.

The truth is, I can't keep a secret. Because I am a recruiter. The truth is you tell me a secret I will tell everyone I know, and then I will begin cold calling.

This is the essence of what I do. I get juicy gossip from clients, masked in the official sounding word we call a job order, and then I spread the juicy gossip to every candidate who can do or knows someone who can do the job, and we call that making recruiting calls. My ability to get the word out like an airborne virus is what has made me successful as a recruiter, and yet it is considered a repellent personal virtue.

"Danny can't keep a secret. I told him I (1) once was in a hotel room getting high when the cops busted in and I snuck out the fire escape, (2) had backstage passes at a Cold Play concert and slipped the drummer's sticks under my jacket, (3) got mad at my Mom and slept with her boyfriend when she went to the store to get pizza I insisted on but didn't really want, it's just that I had this plan and God, I can't believe I'm telling you this..."

Exactly. I get you to tell me. I'm a recruiter. It's like hypnosis. They say you can't hypnotize anyone who doesn't really want to be hypnotized, and I can't get you t tell me anything you don't want me, and everyone I know, to know. This is our nonverbal pact.

You will tell me, and then I will do two things:

189

1) I'll decide who would most enjoy hearing this.
2) I'll polish and edit your story to increase its entertainment value. I do this with integrity. I will not lie. I will not add basic elements. But I will rewrite. It is not my fault if your feeble life pales before my imagination. If you didn't get it right, let me help you.

Most of the time candidates tell you things "in confidence," so that the information can be presented to the hiring authority without them looking greedy, needy, or seedy. You are the middlemen. You take the heat for them. You can always tell the skilled recruiter because they present these concerns as if they are concerns the recruiter would have if the recruiter were the candidate. We depersonalize. We give people ways to gracefully change their minds. Clients say this well. They say, now don't say anything to her about this but my boss, who she is meeting Tuesday, is concerned she hasn't got enough energy. Translation: Tell her to keep up the volume, or she's not going to get the job. And I then relay this "secret" to the candidate, and the candidate performs better. But have I violated some oath to keep a secret? Is this making me a bad person or a phenomenal reader of people's true intentions? And where is the point where you cross over?

After all, in both the Jewish and Christian religions, spreading the Gospel of Gossip is big time Bad. In fact, repeated violations can actually land you in Hell. But this seems absurd to me, since without someone willing to spread rumor and embellish choice gossip, you'd have a hard time getting these religions off the ground.

(Fade in: INT. Dimly lit bar. CAMERA PULLS BACK to reveal two shepherds hanging out.)

SHEPHERD ONE: I'm telling you. Like three guys I know saw it.

SHEPHERD TWO: The whole sea? Parted! You are so full of it!

(OR, Many years later, at the same bar.)

SHEPHERD ONE: I'm telling you, one minute I'm sipping water, this guy waves his hand, next thing I know, I'm bombed. Wine! No stomping. No barrels. Instant wine.

SHEPHERD TWO: So if this guy can do that, why are we sitting here? Let's go find the dude and save some cash.

I don't worry much about the moral or afterlife implications of being a gossip. On my good days, I console myself with the fact that I haven't broken any of the Big Command-ments like killing or stealing, and on my bad days, I just accept that I will be in Hell, and my Type A nature makes me want to take over the place and restructure it before the rest of my recruiters die. I figure we can basically reform the same company for eternity, though how that differs from a recession I don't know.

Do I have a vault? Are there secrets I can keep? Of course. You can convince me that no one can know or else, and I will take a bullet before I will tell anyone. But you have to convince me, and I'm not an easy sell. Because I want to tell everyone.

Here's the good part. Studies have shown that one of the keys to a long life is the inability to conceal. When they took two groups of HIV positive men, the group who stayed in the closet and pretended to have a different illness, died 50% faster than the group who were up front about their illness and about their sexuality. The studies suggest that when you try to keep a secret, you often expend so much energy trying to keep the secret that you drain your mind and spirit.

191

If you live longer and have a fuller spirit by telling secrets, I will no doubt give Moses a run for his money longevitywise, and I will have more spirit in me than the drunk on the Titanic who it is said turned to the bartender and remarked, "I asked for ice, but this is ridiculous."

Non-disclosures? Don't think so. Trade Secret agreement? Save your breath. You hire me to do more than find excellent candidates. In the process of recruiting I am your advertising, your PR, and your corporate communications departments rolled into one. I am your evangelical preacher, and you better fill me with the right Kool Aid, because if you don't, and I get excited, I'll probably start making it up, and as Paul Simon wrote about his Kodachrome... "the pictures never match my sweet imagination, and everything looks worse in black and white."

Oh, speaking of Paul Simon, know what I heard? You can't tell anyone I told you this...

Brother's Keeper

In the Fall of 1985, I was enjoying what Shakespeare called my "salad days" (when I was green with judgment). I was newly single, having divorced my high school sweetheart (she wanted to have kids, I wanted to have other women; it's a long story), twenty-six years old, and the wunderkind of my firm. The chosen one. I had broken all previous production records, and was on track to beat my own record, thanks to one-third Reaganomics and two-thirds Type-A Overdrive. The business consumed m, and when my boss sat me down and said he had a reward for me, only now in retrospect can I see how cheap he was being by offering to send me to a conference in the Poconos. If I offered such a reward to one of my recruiters today, they would resign immediately. But I accepted. Gratefully.

I arrive too late on Friday for any session (had to work all day; now working all day means until lunch!) So I went to my room, changed into casual clothes, and went to the "President's Reception" as a favor to my boss, who wanted me to make an appearance. I knew no one, and so I was forced to stand around with a drink in my hand, feeling awkward, pretending this was on purpose, that this is what I do, pose stiffly in the middle of a room with an expectant smile frozen on my face. Recruiters never really leave high school, and so at parties they hand around in cliques, impenetrable, circumspect.

Then the booming voice of charity. "Hey, brother, whaddaya got, the clap? Or are you just hard to get along with?"

His name was Richie Harris. I didn't read the conference program, so I didn't know that he was one of the speakers. And he never volunteered it. He just said he was a sales recruiter from Westchester County. He bought me a drink. And then another one, and another.

193

I tried to buy him one (cash bard), but he refused. He said, "There's a lot I don't have, money I got."

I told him I usually didn't do the social parts of the conferences, just the sessions. He said he did just the opposite. He introduced me to Tony Byrne, who I had such reverence for I didn't realize he was a real person, by slapping Tony on the back and saying, "Hey, how the f--- do you sleep at night charging $795 for 30 steps? That's like $25 a step. I go to a 12-step program every Tuesday and they don't charge me nothing!" With that, his face erupts, his laugh something between a choke and a chortle. He is, I have since learned, unable to laugh softly; he laughs with energy and fervor, his head tips backwards, he bends t the knees, his eyes widen.

He told me to lighten up, and dared me to have a shot drinking contest. I said that I had to get up early tomorrow for the sessions. He said he did too. He was speaking at 8:00 a.m. I asked him why in the world he would do shots if he had to speak in eight hours. He said he had no choice – nobody in the room had any drugs. And then he questioned my manhood and told me all top producers drink and smoke, and if I didn't choose one he was going to stop hanging with me, and did I remember how popular I was just a little while earlier?

We did shots of whiskey until three in the morning. I found out stuff. He was a boxer as a young man. He was heavily influenced buy his dad, whom he clearly adored, as I did mine. He told me to have kids, to drive a new Mercedes every year, to not take crap from anyone, and to live each day like it was your last, because it could be.

And then I threw up, which he found hysterical. He did another shot, and then helped me to my room. I woke up at 6:00 a.m., and got sick again. I could have slept all day, should have slept all day, but I knew that as much as I was suffering, nothing could compare to feeling the way I did and having to speak for three hours. I showered, threw up, dressed, threw up, and went downstairs for my revenge. I wanted to see this Richie Harris guy suffer.

I walked into his session and put my head, by then green as an archetypal Martian, on the table. I asked everybody to please breathe silently. And then Richie bounded in. He looked like he had just had ten hours of sleep, a light breakfast, and a stirring jog. His face glowed with vigorous health. He walked over to me, put his mouth approximately one quarter inch from my ear and yelled, "Good morning, Mr. Cahill!!!!" Then every time we anted to role play he picked on me.

He spoke for three hours. Cogently. He proved to me you could offer methods and techniques without being boring or dry. And he was insightful. In the same way some people could never recognize Richard Pryor's comic genius because they could not get past his language, there were some in the audience who only heard the occasional profanity, and didn't allow themselves to glean the insight and depth of Richie's knowledge.

In the years that followed, we became close friends. Like all bigger than life characters, we feel nothing can touch them, that they are invincible, and unchanging. I was glad when Richie quit drinking years ago, and a little sad too. I was astonished as I observed him fight his way through divorce and business problems, but I selfishly miss the phone calls where he would tell me about his ex -wife's latest dagger, or the way some client jerked him a round and cost him a deal, because like all truly funny people, they are funnier when they are in pain.

Now I can deal with a down economy. I'm okay with niches shifting and drying up. I can handle how hard we have to work in this market to be profitable. But if I'm going to be a recruiter, I do have some needs. I need Richie Harris healthy. We are, after all, brothers.

ABOUT THE PINNACLE SOCIETY

The Pinnacle Society is the nation's premier consortium of Top Recruiters within the permanent placement and search industry. For more than 15 years, the Pinnacle Society has provided the nation's top recruiters a forum in which to exchange the business principles and placement techniques that lead them to achieve, and allowed them to maintain their success.

The Society only accepts into its membership those persons who:

1) Place candidates permanently on a contingency or contingency/retainer basis for a fee.
2) Have a minimum of five years experience as a Sales Counselor/Manager/Owner in the permanent, contingency or retainer placement business. Non-owners must be nominated for Pinnacle Society membership by his/her owner, or by a Pinnacle Society member.
3) Have cash-in billings in excess of $300,000 annually for three of the past five most recent sales years with one of the last three years showing cash-in billings of more than $400,000.

For more information about the Pinnacle Society, you may go to their Website www.pinnaclesociety.org.

ABOUT DANNY CAHILL AND ACCORDINGTODANNY

Danny Cahill is the only industry "guru" who runs a search firm every day. He does what you do. He has built **Hobson Associates** into one of the country's largest niche search firms, specializing in Sales and Marketing talent for the computer industry. His career personal billings exceed four million dollars and he recently broke the record for the largest fee in his company's history.

In 1990, Danny established the **Cahill Consulting Group**, and began sharing his "hands on" techniques. His dynamic and humorous presentations launched him into immediate prominence. In 1992, '93 and '95, 1997, '98 and '99, his sessions at nationals were the highest rated sessions of the conference. His 1998 keynote, *"Deconstructing Danny,"* and his 2000 keynote are considered landmark events in the industry's history. He has addressed consultants on three continents. His audio and video products are core training tools for thousands of consultants. His Mentoring Program has increased the billings of its participants by over 50%, with new students making their first deals within eight working days.

In October 1995, Danny became the only industry trainer ever asked to speak at a meeting of the **Pinnacle Society**, the top producers in the industry. Over fifty percent of Pinnacle members use Cahill Consulting products. In 1999, the Pinnacle Society appointed him a permanent chairperson's position.

NAPS recently announced a survey calling Danny "their most popular trainer" of all time.

In July of 2002 Danny launched his new Training Company www.AccordingToDanny.com, a website devoted to owners, managers and recruiters. **AccordingToDanny** enables the

199

thousands of recruiters worldwide who have developed their careers through Danny's personal "mentoring" programs or through his renowned series of videos, audio tapes and software products, to have direct access to his guidance "24/7".

His articles have appeared in numerous trade journals and magazines and he has written for CBS television. He received his Master's Degree in literature from Wesleyan University and believes sales people enjoy the world's only job security.